Classics

SWINDON TOWN

FOOTBALL CLUB

Classics

SWINDON TOWN
FOOTBALL CLUB

DICK MATTICK

TEMPUS

First published 2004

Tempus Publishing Limited
The Mill, Brimscombe Port,
Stroud, Gloucestershire, GL5 2QG
www.tempus-publishing.com

British Library Cataloguing in Publication Data.
A catalogue record for this book is available from the British Library.

ISBN 0 7524 2866 7

Typesetting and origination by Tempus Publishing Limited
Printed and bound in Great Britain

Acknowledgements

This book would not have been possible without the input of an awful lot of people. Firstly, I would like to thank all those players and fans, too numerous to mention, who have shared their memories of particular matches with me. I would like to thank Swindon Town FC for a number of things: firstly, for allowing me to reproduce pictures from its programmes; secondly, to Mike Sullivan for allowing me to use the club logo; and last but not least to Mike Spearmen and the directors for giving me access to some of the club's old Minute Books. I would like to thank the *Evening Advertiser* for allowing me to reproduce many of the photographs in this book. The preparation of the book has involved many hours of research in the Swindon Public Library. Despite having to work in conditions that are often cramped compared to many civic libraries the staff have been unfailingly helpful and courteous and have been very kind in providing copies of pictures taken from microfiche and I am extremely grateful to them. Last but not least, Julie Burbidge. Although not a football fan she has the ability to identify how to make the book appeal to a slightly wider audience and has been a most dependable and enthusiastic proofreader. Finally, such faults as remain, and I am sure there are a few, are mine.

Classic Matches

16 January 1908	Sheffield United 2 Swindon Town 3 AET	FA Cup First Round
26 March 1910	Swindon Town 0 Newcastle United 2	FA Cup Semi-Final
25 September 1911	Manchester United 8 Swindon Town 4	FA Charity Shield
30 March 1912	Swindon Town 0 Barnsley 1	FA Cup Semi-Final
28 August 1920	Swindon Town 9 Luton Town 1	Football League Third Division (South)
18 December 1926	Swindon Town 6 Queens Park Rangers 2	Football League Third Division (South)
12 January 1929	Swindon Town 2 Newcastle United 0	FA Cup Third Round
11 January 1930	Manchester United 0 Swindon Town 2	FA Cup Third Round
12 January 1938	Swindon Town 2 Grimsby Town 1 AET	FA Cup Third Round Replay
1 September 1939	Swindon Town 2 Aldershot 2	Football League Third Division (South)
11 January 1947	Swindon Town 5 Watford 0	Football League Third Division (South)
10 January 1948	Burnley 0 Swindon Town 2	FA Cup Third Round
4 February 1952	Stoke City 0 Swindon Town 1	FA Cup Fourth Round Replay
4 May 1955	Swindon Town 2 Reading 0	Football League Third Division (South)
6 December 1958	Swindon Town 1 Norwich City 1	FA Cup Second Round
10 November 1960	Bath City 4 Swindon Town 6	FA Cup First Round Replay
12 January 1963	Swindon Town 5 Queens Park Rangers 0	Football League Third Division
2 March 1963	Swindon Town 3 Bristol City 2	Football League Third Division
14 May 1963	Swindon Town 1 Shrewsbury Town 0	Football League Third Division
24 September 1963	Swindon Town 3 Chelsea 0	Football League Cup Second Round
27 April 1964	Swindon Town Youths 1 Manchester United Youths 1	FA Youth Cup Final First Leg
23 March 1965	Swindon Town 4 Northampton Town 2	Football League Second Division

24 April 1965	Southampton 2 Swindon Town 1	Football League Second Division
28 January 1967	West Ham United 3 Swindon Town 3	FA Cup Third Round
26 November 1968	Northampton Town 2 Swindon Town 6	Football League Third Division
18 December 1968	Swindon 3 Burnley 3	Football League Cup Semi-Final Replay
15 March 1969	Swindon Town 3 Arsenal 1 AET	Football League Cup Final
28 May 1970	Napoli 0 Swindon Town 3	Anglo-Italian Cup Final
6 October 1970	Swindon Town 2 Liverpool 0	Football League Cup Third Round
13 January 1972	Swindon Town 2 Birmingham City 0	FA Cup Third Round
29 January 1977	Swindon Town 2 Everton 2	FA Cup Fourth Round
26 December 1977	Oxford United 3 Swindon Town 3	Football League Third Division
24 February 1979	Rotherham 1 Swindon Town 3	Football League Third Division
8 December 1979	Swindon Town 8 Bury 0	Football League Third Division
11 December 1979	Swindon Town 4 Arsenal 3 AET	Football League Cup Fifth Round Replay
18 May 1982	Newport County 1 Swindon Town 0	Football League Third Division
7 April 1986	Swindon Town 4 Chester City 2	Football League Fourth Division
14 May 1987	Wigan Athletic 2 Swindon Town 3	Football League Third Division Play-Off Semi-Final First Leg
29 May 1987	Gillingham 0 Swindon Town 2	Football League Third Division Play-Off Final
28 May 1990	Sunderland 0 Swindon Town 1	Football League Second Division Play-Off Final
12 April 1993	Birmingham City 4 Swindon Town 6	Football League Division One
31 May 1993	Leicester City 3 Swindon Town 4	Football League Division One Play-Off Final
11 December 1993	Liverpool 2 Swindon Town 2	FA Premier League
19 March 1994	Swindon Town 2 Manchester United 2	FA Premier League
11 January 1995	Swindon Town 3 Millwall 1	Football League Cup Fifth Round
20 April 1996	Blackpool 1 Swindon Town 1	Football League Division Two
5 November 1997	Swindon Town 3 Queens Park Rangers 1	Football League Division One
28 April 2001	Swindon Town 2 Peterborough United 1	Football League Division Two
13 October 2001	Reading 1 Swindon Town 3	Football League Division Two
10 August 2002	Swindon Town 3 Barnsley 1	Football League Division Two

Introduction

Having to select fifty matches from the many that Swindon Town FC have played during their long history has not been easy. Some matches are clearly musts, such as the three Wembley triumphs, while others are there for the quality of the football played regardless of the impact on the club's destiny. Any selection must to some extent be subjective and the fact that I have watched thirty-two of them indicates that I have leant towards the last fifty years. I have, however, tried to make sure that all periods of the club's history are covered and that the sequence of matches covers the fluctuating fortunes it has endured throughout its existence. As you read through the pages of this book you will come across the highest-scoring Charity Shield match ever, a game where Harry Morris scored five goals and Swindon's last match before their ground was turned into a prisoner-of-war camp. Moving into the post-war period the club's many successes as giant-killers feature heavily before we reach the first League promotion campaign of 1962/63. I have included three matches from this period but, as with the later periods of success under Lou Macari and Glenn Hoddle, many excellent matches have been omitted to obtain a balance between the many eras of the Robins' story.

Besides telling the story of the actual matches I have tried to set them in context, explaining the club's situation when the games were played and, where appropriate, something of the national picture during the period in which the match took place. Several matches include outstanding individual performances and where this is the case I have tried to say something about the methods that contributed to the individual's success, while others are stories of team triumphs, often in the face of adversity. The latter type of match is well illustrated by the Wembley final where despite the heartbreak of conceding a last-minute equaliser Town battled back to prove, in the words of Geoffrey Green, 'that all the wealth of Arsenal could not match the gold of Swindon's courage'. Before closing this introduction I would like to quote some words of J.B. Priestley about spectators and football: 'To say that these men paid their shillings to watch twenty-two hirelings kick a ball is merely to say that a violin is wood and catgut, that *Hamlet* is so much paper and ink.' For generations of Town followers, Swindon's games have provided not only conflict and art but myriad memories. After a disappointing defeat, or in the summer when the new season seems far away, turn the pages of this book to live again the glories of yesteryear and the Robins of old.

SHEFFIELD UNITED V. SWINDON TOWN

Sheffield United 2 Swindon Town 3 AET
FA Cup First Round 16 January 1908

United won the toss and elected to play so that Swindon would have the sun in their eyes. The crowd included a 'good sprinkling of Swindonians', later reckoned at about 400, a sizeable contingent when one remembers that replays took place with less than a week's notice and time off work was not always easy to obtain. Sheffield opened with an attack down the right but the tackling of Jock Walker prevented any breakthrough. Harold Fleming, later to become almost a fixture in the number eight shirt, was playing at outside left in this game and it was following a fine run by him that Warburton was given the opportunity to score and repay the faith his captain had shown in him earlier in the day. Johnston twice tried to increase Swindon's lead with long shots but Leivesley dealt with them competently. Rushton was a bustling presence for Swindon in midfield and his excellent passing was proving something of a handful for the United players. Fleming broke through and might have increased Swindon's lead had he not been pulled up for offside. Ling, in the Swindon goal, was brought into action, producing two fine saves from Lipsham. When Gill ran the ball out of defence for Swindon he was dispossessed by Brown just as the move began to look threatening. Rain began to fall just before the interval and with the Sheffield smog lowering above the ground the unreal atmosphere seemed to match the unreality of the fact that a First Division side was being dominated by the team from the Southern League.

Sheffield began the second half seemingly intent on putting the natural order of things back in place. A cross by Hardinge was fastened on to by Lipsham but, for a third time in the match, he was foiled by Ling. A corner for the Blades five minutes into the half led to a scrimmage in the goalmouth with Brown eventually turning the ball into the Town net. Swindon hit back quickly and in the words of one reporter after a clever run by Fleming, the Sheffield 'keeper 'only just saved his citadel'. Then came a crucial incident. A nasty charge by Brown laid out Walker. The referee, Mr Heath, administered a caution and after a lengthy delay for treatment to the Swindon full-back, the game resumed. The tough Scot was clearly in trouble however. He gallantly tackled one Sheffield player but was unable to regain his feet and a fellow defender had to hack the ball away at the expense of a corner. This was partly cleared but Lipsham gained possession and, at last, beat Ling from a narrow angle. Walker reluctantly limped from the fray and many must have felt that with him went Swindon's hopes. Johnston for Swindon and Bromage for Sheffield both missed chances before Bromage again put the ball in the net for United. However, Walker's absence meant Swindon were playing a one-back defence and this had provided an offside trap which ruled out the 'goal' on the grounds of offside. Swindon gained a throw on the left and the ball was transferred to the right where it found Tout. With more Sheffield players around him than Swindon ones he tried in desperation a pot shot that slipped through the hands of Leivesley to level the scores.

The full-time whistle blew with the scores still level but a debate took place before the resumption. The light now was decidedly murky and Swindon objected to the game continuing. Whether this was a genuine concern about the light, a desire to fight another day with a full strength XI or just the pecuniary interest of another gate to boost the finances we shall probably never know, but it was decided by Mr Heath that the game should continue. Following a treatment not commonly used by physios today, the rubbing of whisky into the injured leg, Walker returned to

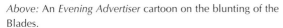

Above: An *Evening Advertiser* cartoon on the blunting of the Blades.

Right: Jock Walker – the Town full-back who received unusual medical treatment during the match.

the fray but now at inside left in an unlikely pairing with Harold Fleming, the man who in years to come would line up on the opposite side in England *v.* Scotland matches. Sheffield had the better of the first session of extra time but the best chance came to Swindon near its end. Fleming cleverly beat a defender but, before he could shoot, Leivesley snatched the ball from his feet. Warburton proved Town's saviour earlier in the second period of extra time, stopping a Bromage effort on the line with his head. In the days of the heavy balls that soaked up water, this was a courageous feat and he required treatment before continuing. Then came what was to be the deciding goal, a magnificent shot by Johnston. Shortly after the final whistle blew, the sporting Sheffield side congratulated their opponents on victory in what had been a magnificent cup tie.

The great Harold Fleming identified this match as the turning point in the club's history and the game that made them believe that they could compete with the best.

Sheffield United: Leivesley; Benson, Johnston; W.H. Wilkinson, D. Wilkinson, Needham; Thompson, Hardinge, Brown, Bromage, Lipsham.
Swindon Town: Ling; Gill, Walker; Tout, Bannister, Chambers; Johnson, Lyon, Rushton, Warburton, Fleming.
Attendance: 19,566

Swindon Town v. Newcastle United

Swindon Town 0 Newcastle United 2
FA Cup Semi-Final 26 March 1910

When the draw for the FA Cup semi-final paired Swindon with Newcastle United the *Evening Advertiser* proudly pointed out that it kept their forecast of a final in 'the shadow of the great glasshouse' at Sydenham between Swindon and Everton alive. It certainly set Swindon a tough task as the Tynesiders had reached the penultimate round for the fifth time in five years having overcome Stoke, Fulham, Blackburn and Leicester Fosse on the way, scoring 13 goals and conceding just 3. Although they had had to play just one away match, winning 3-1 at Crystal Palace, Swindon had already faced tough opposition, beating Burnley, Tottenham and Manchester City to reach their first ever semi-final.

The match was played at Tottenham's ground and no fewer than four excursion trains were run by the Great Western Railway to take fans to the game, where it was estimated that the Newcastle fans were outnumbered by two to one. The scene that greeted these fans was a very different one to the County Ground, the White Hart Lane ground looking enormous by comparison with a large new stand and huge mounds for standing spectators. One way it did not compare favourably with the County Ground was the condition of the pitch. This was described as being 'innocent of grass' apart from a few tufts around the corner flags and goalmouths. The game was to provide a great clash of styles, with Newcastle's game being built around passing while Swindon were described as 'each man a unit not a part of the whole'. This was probably a reference to the individual dribbling style best exemplified by Town's legendary inside right Harold Fleming. The stretcher bearers were called on to remove several people who fainted, which probably indicates that even this large ground was straining to cope with the crowd, and a reporter's comment that the cinematographic men were busy indicates at least some film was taken of the match and one wonders if it has survived. It had been a cloudy day. The sun broke through, just as Bannister led Swindon Town onto the field in what was seen by many Swindon optimists as a good omen.

Swindon won the toss but the opening attacks came from the Magpies. Howie headed wide and then 'a rush by Higgins was halted by Kay'. Swindon's best chance in the first half came after some brilliant skill by Fleming ended with a centre to Billy Silto, whose shot was saved at the expense of a corner. Another example of the individual nature of much of Swindon's play is provided by the fact that the *Evening Advertiser* report notes how 'Bown was brought down having run half the length of the pitch'. The first half seems to have been a very evenly matched struggle with saves by Len Skiller in the Swindon goal alternating with corners for Swindon being frittered away.

The second half saw the swift inter-passing of the Newcastle team building pressure on the Swindon goal. Swindon came close to breaking the deadlock in the sixtieth minute when former schoolmaster Freddie Wheatcroft saw his shot strike the post. Ten minutes later, Rutherford received the ball from a free-kick and, before Walker could tackle, hit a rising shot into the Swindon goal off the underside of the crossbar. Two minutes later Rutherford passed the ball to Stewart, who placed his shot into the Town goal. Swindon had evidently been the underdogs as one report spoke of 'the sturdy determined railwaymen and the brilliant Tynesiders' but until this spell of two goals in three minutes they had equalled the Geordies. Desperation now set in and with Newcastle happy to pass the ball around to keep possession, and Swindon rushing around in the knowledge that time was

Swindon players of 1909/10. Working from left to right, top row to bottom row: Skiller, Chambers, Hemmings, Kay, Mansell, Walker, Dibsdall, Tout, Bannister, Fleming, Silto, Saunders, Jefferson, Innes, Lamb, Fenton, McCulloch, Wheatcroft, Bown, Bolland.

running out, the Robins never looked like getting back into the match. The reporter 'Corinthian' summed it up by writing 'Newcastle's win was the triumph of footballing science over magnificent determination. Swindon succeeded in making a close game of it with a far superior side, and when that is fairly done there is no greater merit to be gained in football or any other sport.'

Among the notable performers in the Swindon team were Skiller the goalkeeper, who had saved several close-range shots, though goalkeeping purists would blanch at the comment that 'he used his fists to good effect'; Scottish international full-back Jock Walker who had made numerous vital interventions in 'rough and tumbles around the Swindon goal'; and thirdly Billy Silto, who was noted for his excellent work not only in defence but in feeding his forwards.

Swindon Town: Skiller; Kay, Walker; Tout, Bannister, Silto; Jefferson, Fleming, Wheatcroft, Bown, Lavery.

Newcastle United: Lawrence; Whitson, McCracken; McWilliam, Low, Veitch; Wilson, Higgins, Shepherd, Howie, Rutherford.

Attendance: 40,000

An *Evening Advertiser* cartoon from days leading up to the cup semi-final. 'Tottenham' on the flowerpot refers to Spurs being beaten 1-0 in the previous round.

MANCHESTER UNITED V. SWINDON TOWN

Manchester United 8 Swindon Town 4
FA Charity Shield 25 September 1911

Nowadays, the Charity Shield is competed for by the winners of the Premiership and the winners of the FA Cup. In pre-war days, the selection of the teams seems to have been more varied and in 1911 Manchester United, the winners of the League, had Swindon Town, winners of the Southern League, as their opponents. Unlike today, when the match is the curtain-raiser of the season, the season was already three weeks old when the match took place at Chelsea's Stamford Bridge ground. Swindon played in their traditional red shirts while Manchester United changed into blue ones. Swindon kicked towards 'the road goal' and enjoyed the best of the early exchanges, with Lamb forcing a corner and Silto forcing a good save from Edmonds. They took the lead when Freddie Wheatcroft moved onto the left wing and centred for Harold Fleming to score with a header. The lead was short-lived as United struck back by equalising immediately, with Turnball shooting into the corner of the net. After twenty minutes, Manchester United went in front. Halse rounded Town full-back Kay and shot past Len Skiller. The game was a fast-flowing exhibition of football skills and Town nearly levelled the scores when Archie Bown put in a strong shot which Edmonds just managed to hang on to. There was a note of controversy about United's third goal, when Halse tapped in from close range, as he appeared to be in front of Wall, from whom he received the pass. However, after consulting the linesman, referee Schumacher allowed the goal to stand. Town's right-winger 'Shuffler Jeff', as he was sometimes called, made a fine run before crossing the ball which Wheatcroft dived down to head, reducing the deficit to one. Halse completed his hat-trick, a fine feat, but one that was to pale in comparison to what he was to achieve by the end of this match. Freddie Wheatcroft, who would sadly be killed only four years later during the fighting in France, was having a grand match. He had been involved in Town's first two goals and now, being pulled down by Holton, won the penalty which Tout converted to complete the first-half scoring.

Given the rate that goals had been going in, it was remarkable that ten minutes of the second half elapsed without a goal, but then the Wall-Halse combination struck again, Halse scoring with what the *Advertiser* reporter described as 'the best goal of the match'. Two more goals came from Halse to end the game as a contest before Wall added United's eighth goal. Swindon continued to contribute to the entertainment, though there was a shade of fortune about the last goal, a shot from Jefferson that Edmonds went down to gather, only for the ball to kick up off the turf and glance off his shoulder into the net. Sir C. Wakefield presented medals to both sides after a game contested in glorious weather that few who saw it will ever forget and which still stands as the record aggregate score for a Charity Shield match.

The absence of Jock Walker, due to illness, had forced Town to reorganise their defence and may account for the large number of goals conceded. Tout took over Walker's left-back position but reports indicate he was not comfortable away from his normal right half position and that Kay seemed unsettled by the lack of his normal partner. Perhaps most importantly of all, the reshuffle saw Charlie Bannister brought back into the team. One of the longest-serving Town players, he was still a doughty campaigner but now was, perhaps, past his best. He was given the centre-half berth that would normally have been occupied by Billy Silto, whose greater speed might have enabled him to exercise more control over Halse.

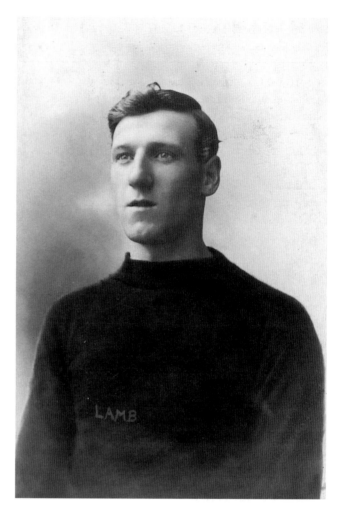

Town left-winger Sammy Lamb. Born in Alfreton in 1886, he made 30 League appearances for Derby. Later he joined Swindon Town from Plymouth Argyle. Swindon sold him to Millwall Athletic and he ended his League career after the First World War with Rotherham.

Manchester United: Edmonds; Hopton, Stacey; Duckworth, Roberts, Bell; Meredith, Hamill, Halse, Turnball, Wall.

Swindon Town: Skiller; Kay, Tout; Handley, Bannister, Silto; Jefferson, Fleming, Wheatcroft, Bown, Lamb.

Attendance: 12,000

SWINDON TOWN v. BARNSLEY

Swindon Town 0 Barnsley 1
FA Cup Semi-Final 30 March 1912

In 1910 the two defeated Cup semi-finalists, Swindon and Barnsley, were invited by the French footballing authorities to play at the Parc des Princes for the Dubonnet Trophy. Two goals from Harold Fleming were enough for Swindon to win the match 2-1 and so be awarded the largest if not the most expensive trophy the club has ever won. Two years later, the sides met again in the FA Cup, often known at the time as the English Cup. On their way to the semi-final, Barnsley had conceded just four goals and had only overcome the cup holders after three goalless draws in a tie that lasted over seven hours. Swindon's route to the final had begun with an easy 5-0 victory over Sutton Junction and proceeded with victories over Notts County, West Ham and, most notably of all, Everton. Everton had the legendary Irish international Elisha Scott in goal, Harry Makepeace, an English international at both football and cricket, and Tom 'Boy' Browell, who Swindon's Billy Silto reckoned had the most powerful shot he had ever seen. Despite this, Bob Jefferson and Archie Bown scored in the opening twenty minutes and Town hung on to win 2-1.

A crowd of 48,057 saw the two sides play out a 0-0 draw at Stamford Bridge. Fleming was constantly hacked down and, on one occasion, kneed in the groin. The *Daily Express* commented that 'Barnsley's treatment of one of the cleanest players that ever lived was quite disgraceful. To stop a clever opponent by maiming him is not football as we know it in the South'. So badly injured was he that he missed not only the replay but the rest of the season. Bryon Butler in his book *The Giantkillers* described Barnsley as laying into Swindon 'like foxes in a chicken run'. The fact that there is nothing new in the idea of a sin bin is shown by the fact that a correspondent rejoicing under the name of 'Cross Stick' suggested that players that fouled persistently, as some of the Barnsley ones did, should have to spend a period out of the game sitting on the touchline thus earning the displeasure of their teammates. The replay at Meadow Lane saw Swindon include Burtinshaw in place of the injured Fleming and the *Advertiser* commented that Swindon might be 'greatly impaired' by the loss of the forward, who had been 'badly crippled by his adversaries at Chelsea' and hoped that the 'dash and vigour' of Burtinshaw might be worth more in a match in which skilful football was likely to be at a premium. As it happened, an even more crucial omission from the team was that of Billy Tout. He was the team's regular penalty taker. Swindon were awarded a penalty in the first half and Billy Silto, perhaps anxious to get on the scoresheet against his old club, stepped up to take it. 'You don't take penalties' said Peter Chambers, who was not only replacing Tout as a wing half but also as skipper, and the kick was taken by Archie Bown. He struck the kick well but it was brilliantly saved by Cooper. Ten minutes into the second half, Skiller conceded a corner. Bartrop took it and Bratley, who had come up from defence, headed it in. Barnsley went on to win the Cup, defeating West Bromwich just as they had Swindon, scoring the only goal in a replay after the first match had been goalless.

Swindon Town: Skiller; Kay, Walker; Handley, Silto, Chambers; Jefferson, Burtinshaw, Wheatcroft, Bown, Bolland.

Barnsley: Cooper; Downs, Taylor; Glendinning, Bratley, Utley; Bertrop, Tufnell, Lillycrop, Travers, Moore.

Attendance: 18,000

SWINDON TOWN v. BARNSLEY

Above: The Barnsley squad that defeated Swindon and went on to win the cup.

Opposite above: Cartoon comment on the methods by which Barnsley achieved their victory. The word 'Swindon' is just visible on the schoolboy's cap.

Opposite below: Swindon Town's squad for the 1911/12 season. From left to right, back row: Padfield, Kay, Skiller, Walker, Woolford. Middle row: Sam Allen (secretary), Warman (assistant trainer), Ruston, Tout, Bannister, Silto, Handley, Wiltshire (trainer). Front row: Jefferson, Fleming, Wheatcroft, Burkinshaw, McCullock, Bown, Lamb, Bolland.

Swindon Town v. Luton Town

Swindon Town 9 Luton Town 1
Football League Third Division (South) 28 August 1920

In 1920 the Football League decided that the Southern League should become the Third Division (South) with automatic promotion and relegation into the Second Division, albeit for only one club. Cardiff City, who had been the Southern League champions, were promoted to the Second Division, but otherwise Swindon's opposition in their first season in League football was what it had been in the Southern League.

The Gorse Hill Brass Band played what were described as 'inspiring' tunes as an expectant crowd gathered. By the time Harold Fleming led out the Swindon players not far short of 10,000 were estimated to be in the crowd for the match, which had a 3.30 p.m. kick-off. Swindon were without Len Skiller, who had a thigh strain, but an up-and-coming youngster, Ted Nash, who in years to come would be the first Swindon player to be ever-present during a Football League season, was an admirable deputy.

Luton won the toss and decided to attack the Stratton End. The *Evening Advertiser* reported that 'at the outset Luton showed sparkling form, but Swindon wore them down.' This was to prove a classic understatement by the game's end. Batty tested Watson early in the game and the Hatters' 'keeper held the shot that was going over his head. Winger Jefferson put over a fine cross, but nobody was on hand to turn it home. A clearance kick by Kay found Wareing, who laid the ball off to Dave Rogers. The Swindon centre forward engaged in a neat exchange of passes with Batty who shot low into the corner to claim the honour of being the first Town player to score a League goal.

Neither the *Evening Advertiser* of the match day, the report of which ended at half-time, nor the following Monday edition, or indeed the weekly *Swindon Advertiser* reported on the second-half avalanche of goals. However, it is interesting that they then announced that a special football edition would be issued at 6.00 p.m. and a football special issued at 6.45 p.m. in future weeks. The Monday *Advertiser* contained some general remarks that tells us a little more of the players' performance. The local reporter of the time, who rejoiced under the name 'Observer', felt that 'the Luton defence was not of the same kidney as that of previous years' but attributed the Town's victory to the fact that they had 'used their brains as well as their feet'. Dave Rogers was singled out as showing 'rare skill and intelligence'. The comment on Fleming's goals was muddling and less easy to follow, describing how the England international, who scored four times, 'made scoring look like child's play but were goals that only Fleming could have scored'. Jefferson was hailed as having 'a sparkling game and made full use of the opportunities provided him by Fleming'. The *Daily Telegraph* described how Luton were hopelessly outclassed, while the *Daily Express* stated that 'Swindon's old brigade proved their football careers were a long way from over' and the *Sporting Life* felt Swindon were 'in a class by themselves in pace and skill'. The remarkable nature of football is shown by the fact that within a week of what to this day is their biggest League victory, Swindon lost twice. The second defeat was to the Luton team that they had beaten just seven days earlier!

Swindon Town: Nash; Kay, Macconachie; Langford, Hawley, Wareing; Jefferson, Fleming, Rogers, Batty, Davies.
Luton Town: Watson; Lennon, Semple; Roe, Lamb, Parker; J.L. Bradley, Pett, E.F. Bradley, Mathieson, Bookman.

THIRD DIVISION

		P	W	D	L	F	A	Pts
1	Crystal Palace	42	24	11	7	70	34	59
2	Southampton	42	19	16	7	64	28	54
3	QPR	42	22	9	11	61	32	53
4	Swindon	42	21	10	11	73	49	52
5	Swansea	42	18	15	9	56	45	51
6	Watford	42	20	8	14	59	44	48
7	Millwall Ath	42	18	11	13	42	30	47
8	Merthyr Town	42	15	15	12	60	49	45
9	Luton	42	16	12	14	61	56	44
10	Bristol Rovers	42	18	7	17	68	57	43
11	Plymouth	42	11	21	10	35	34	43
12	Portsmouth	42	12	15	15	46	48	39
13	Grimsby	42	15	9	18	49	59	39
14	Northampton	42	15	8	19	59	75	38
15	Newport	42	14	9	19	43	64	37
16	Norwich	42	10	16	16	44	53	36
17	Southend	42	14	8	20	44	61	36
18	Brighton	42	14	8	20	42	61	36
19	Exeter	42	10	15	17	39	54	35
20	Reading	42	12	7	23	42	59	31
21	Brentford	42	9	12	21	42	67	30
22	Gillingham	42	8	12	22	34	74	28

Above left: Harold Fleming, who scored four goals in Swindon's first ever Football League match.

Above right: A League table showing Swindon in fourth position at the end of their first ever season of League Football, 1920/21. It was known as the Third Division rather than the Third Division (South), as the Third Division (North) was not created until the following season.

SWINDON TOWN v. QUEENS PARK RANGERS

Swindon Town 6 Queens Park Rangers 2
Football League Third Division (South) 18 December 1926

Between 6 November and 28 December 1926, Swindon Town enjoyed a run in which they won eight consecutive League matches. Perhaps the finest victory in this run was that over Queens Park Rangers. Swindon took the field as league leaders, having defeated Crystal Palace 6-1 at the County Ground and Aberdare Athletic 4-1 in Wales in their previous games. Swindon were able to turn out an unchanged team. In the Queens Park Rangers side at centre half was Fred Hawley, who had made 90 League appearances for Town earlier in the twenties before moving to Bristol City, from where he had joined Queens Park Rangers.

Swindon attacked the Town end in the first half with a stiff breeze at their backs and a crowd estimated at not more than 5,000, who at kick-off were still making their way into the ground. The first goal to be threatened was Town's but Charlesworth, having received a centre, was just off target. Swindon hit back and Denyer and Wall combined to win a corner that was wasted when it was put straight out behind the goal, Denyer perhaps not having allowed enough for the wind. Moments later, Morris was forced to leave the field after colliding with Cunningham in the Queens Park Rangers goal. How the Londoners must have wished he had stayed off. Shortly after returning to the field, Harry Morris burst through the middle only to be fouled just outside the area. Danny Bew came up to take the kick and placed a fine high kick into the path of Alec Wall, who ran on to head home from an angle. Cunningham produced saves from Eddleston and Morris before, against the run of play, Goddard scored, shooting home from a cross with a hard, low shot. Swindon's lead was soon restored by Morris who 'gallantly broke through and scored in great style'. The Swindon leader was having a 'splendid game' and fired a glorious drive that Cunningham went full length to save. Morris' second, and Swindon's third, came with a shot from a good distance that struck the post and found its way into the net.

The second half started with Morris still in rampant form, storming through several opponents and beating Cunningham with a shot that went narrowly wide. The *Football Pink* report described Bertie Denyer and Harry Morris as Town's two outstanding men, and it was a cross by the former that was headed in by the latter to complete his hat-trick. Morris scored his fourth bursting onto a through ball. The Queens Park Rangers side were aggrieved that the goal was allowed to stand and play was held up for a couple of minutes while they protested that Morris was offside. They showed their displeasure in the period that followed through 'rough charging and wild kicking', but it had no effect on the Town forwards. 'Give it to Morris' was a frequent chant of the period, but this was being forsaken by the crowd who were now voicing the number of goals scored in case the Rangers players were in any doubt. An historic fifth goal came when a Joe Eddleston shot had been beaten out by the Rangers 'keeper and Morris fastened onto the ball and dribbled in from a wide angle before shooting home. It was the first time a Swindon player had scored five goals in a Football League match, a feat that no other player has subsequently achieved, although Morris himself did it again and Keith East scored five in a cup tie. Swindon might have got a seventh goal had not the referee missed a clear case of hands, but with victory in the bag Town took something of a breather. As Rangers came back into the game, Wally Dickenson and 'Tober' Weston dealt with most of the threats but Lofthouse did manage to elude them and find Goddard with a centre. Goddard's effort

Above: The Swindon squad for the 1926/27 season. Morris is in the front row. Someone has written O's on his chest, no doubt as he joined Clapton Orient in 1933.

Right: A newspaper headline celebrating the five-goal achievement of Harry Morris.

THE HAT TRICK—AND THEN SOME!

Morris Again Demonstrates Art of Goal-getting.

ANOTHER SMASHING SUCCESS.

beat Bourne in the Town goal despite the latter's full-length dive. For Alec Wall the goal he scored in this match would be his last for Swindon as he sustained a broken leg in a later match with Merthyr. This injury to their midfield schemer halted Town's run of success and their promising promotion challenge faded.

Swindon Town: Bourne; Dickenson, Weston; Cooper, Bew, Archer; Denyer, Wall, Morris, Eddleston, Thom.
Queens Park Rangers: Cunningham; Pierce, Young; McAllister, Hawley, Middleton; Mustard, Charlesworth, Goddard, Burgess, Lofthouse.
Attendance: 6,706

Swindon Town v. Newcastle United

Swindon Town 2 Newcastle United 0
FA Cup Third Round 12 January 1929

In the words of the *Evening Advertiser*, Swindon were 'bonny cup fighters the previous year'. Although only in the Third Division (South), Swindon were exempt from this competition until the Third Round. This brought them a plum home tie against Newcastle United. Swindon came alive on cup day with Newcastle fans arriving at the County Ground as early as eight in the morning. The Newcastle team had stayed at Weston-super-Mare overnight and travelled up to Swindon that morning, before enjoying a lunch at the Railway Hotel. The County Ground had been prepared for the big day with goalposts and boards freshly painted. The pitch itself had required a considerable amount of attention with a heavy roller being needed to flatten the frosty pitch. Anticipating a big crowd, many fans had arrived at the ground early and were entertained by the Great Western Railway Prize Band.

The sun was shining brightly, but it was still bitterly cold as a biting north-east wind was blowing. Having won the toss, Town skipper Wally Dickenson decided to kick against the wind in the first half, leaving the visitors to face the sun. An entertaining opening period of play saw each side attack in turn but no chances of note were created. The first real opportunity came when Bertie Denyer beat his man, but he delayed his shot just too long, allowing Harris to clear. An error by Dickenson let in the Scottish wizard Hughie Gallacher, and Swindon fans had their hearts in their mouths until Wylie's timely tackle saved the day. Ted Nash punched a centre clear as Newcastle pressure began to mount. Swindon's short passing was a bit too intricate for the conditions. Newcastle, on the other hand, showed some good approach play, but were let down by some sloppy finishing. This, it has to be said, was not due to Gallacher. Danny Bew was keeping such a tight grip on the international that he scarcely had the chance to get a sight of goal. In contrast, Harry Morris was showing the dash and powers of leadership which had endeared him to Swindon fans since he joined their club from Swansea. He had twice unsettled the Magpies' defence with speedy bursts before he created and scored the goal that put Town in front. Gaining possession on the edge of the area, he dribbled to the right before going back towards goal, beating Thomas and shooting home. In an event rare at the time, a Swindon fan came out of the crowd and ran onto the field to embrace him. The fan was shepherded away but it was some moments before play could resume as the Swindon players were celebrating too. Undaunted by the reception, Morris was soon in action again and it required good work by Maitland to prevent a further goal. Swindon had Newcastle on the ropes now and Eddleston forced another save with a shot that was going just under the bar. With the cold of the elements and the heat of the Swindon pressure, the Newcastle players must have been glad to reach the sanctuary of the dressing room at half-time.

With the addition of the wind at their backs, the Swindon players proved irresistible in the second half. Not only did they hold their lead, they increased it. Morris was the scorer with, unusually for him, a header. When Newcastle did attack, they found a superb pair of full-backs in Dickenson and Wylie and the work of Nash in goal always inspired confidence. However, the game nearly ended on an unhappy note. An overly robust charge left Alec Thom the Swindon winger injured after a collision with the board around the pitch, but the injury did not prove as serious as was at first feared. Harris, the Newcastle skipper, was man enough to admit 'the best team had won'. A tough

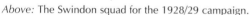

Above: The Swindon squad for the 1928/29 campaign.

Right: Scottish International Hughie Gallacher, who was well contained by the Swindon defence.

draw rewarded Town with a trip to Burnley, which they came through by beating the Lancashire side 3-2 at the County Ground after a 3-3 draw away. An even tougher match in the fifth round saw them drawn against Arsenal. They held the Gunners to a draw at the County Ground but lost at Highbury to the only goal of the game.

Swindon Town: Nash; Dickenson, Wylie; Low, Bew, Archer; Denyer, Eddleston, Morris, Roberts, Thom.
Newcastle United: Burns; Maitland, Thomas; Carlton, Park, Harris; Urwin, Boyd, Gallacher, McCurley, Lang.
Attendance: 17,689

Manchester United v. Swindon Town

Manchester United 0 Swindon Town 2
FA Cup Third Round 11 January 1930

There is an old saying that 'in the cup, League form goes out of the window'. This was never better illustrated than in this match. Swindon, a Third Division side at the time, had played 11 away games without a single win and with only 2 draws to show for their efforts. Even their presence in the third round was due to the previous season, when they had reached the fifth round and thus gained exemption until the third round. Failure had brought the usual letters to the press and even the legendary Morris had not escaped criticism, with some suggesting that Dent should take his place. Their opponents Manchester United, though not the lofty power of today, were a solid First Division team and even the normally optimistic local press was sanguine about the prospects, stating 'a draw is not outside the realms of possibility, but that is as much as can be hoped for'. Despite this, some 600 supporters, most of them on a GWR special, made the journey north. Swindon fielded a full-strength side with the exception of Alec Thom, who had been sidelined since September with a back injury. Playing Dent was not an option, as he had, according to trainer Wiltshire, who was evidently not into medical terminology, 'a groggy ankle'.

The game opened with a Roberts cross from which Morris made a characteristic dash which was only just checked by Moore. At the other end, Girvan checked one United attack before United's Jones fired a long shot wide. The first real 'heart in the mouth' moment came when Denyer sent over a cross that was met by McCartney, whose header was snatched from under the bar by the home 'keeper. There was an air of amazement reflected in the comment that 'Swindon was the superior side in the opening ten minutes'. A cross from McCartney caused a melee in the Manchester United goal, but Swindon were soon under the cosh with Spence and Boyle forcing saves from Ted Nash, while Girvan had to leave the field after a collision in which he had suffered a knock to the forehead. This was plastered up before he returned to the fray. The best chance of the first half fell to Bertie Denyer but, when he had just the 'keeper to beat, he skied his shot over the bar. On twenty-nine minutes came a goal that stunned most of the crowd but led to ecstatic celebrations among the Swindon contingent. Joe Eddleston received the ball, following a throw from McCartney, at the edge of the United area and fired it into the net 'like a shot from a gun'. United were momentarily stunned and good work by McCartney set up Morris but his shot was saved. United rallied and in the five minutes before half-time Nash did well first to turn a shot by Boyle over the bar and then to turn an effort by Rowley round the post.

Swindon's second-half hero was Ted Nash, who pulled off a string of fine saves as Manchester United piled on the pressure. Swindon had that little bit of luck that any side needs in a cup tie, with the ball twice rebounding from their woodwork. Swindon extended their lead, however, when Bertie Denyer produced a fine run before crossing to Roberts, who headed home.

After the match the Manchester United directors asked if Bertie, who they described as the kid on the wing, was available for transfer. Denyer, who was thirty-six at the time and had lost half his intestines due to a First World War injury, thought this a great joke. By this time he was combining his football with acting as steward at the High Street Club and was settled enough in Swindon. A quirk of fate saw Swindon drawn against the other team from Manchester, this time

Jo Eddleston, scorer of one of the goals in Town's surprise victory at Old Trafford.

Bertie Denyer,
the other scorer.

with home advantage. However, Swindon failed to progress. Although a 1-1 draw earned another bumper pay day (the gate of 46,082 being larger than that at Old Trafford) it also led to a record cup defeat with Harry Morris scoring a solitary goal for Town in reply to ten by their opponents in the replay at Maine Road.

Manchester United: Stewart; Moore, Jones; Hilditch, Taylor, Wilson; Spence, Boyle, Taylor, Rowley, McLachlan.

Swindon Town: Nash; Penn, Girvan; Low, Humphries, Archer; Denyer, Eddleston, Morris, Roberts, McCartney.

Attendance: 33,226

" DADDY " BALL'S DREAM.

"Daddy" Ball, the 80-year-old grounds-man of the Swindon F.C., has dreamed that the Town will win 5—2 on Satur-day, and his cheeriness is shown in the picture. Daddy with some of the Swindon players.

'Daddy' Ball, who was the groundsman at Swindon for twenty years, eventually retiring at the age of eighty, dreamt that Swindon would win at Old Trafford by five goals to two. He got the scoreline wrong but he was right about the win.

Swindon Town v. Grimsby Town

Swindon Town 2 Grimsby Town 1 AET
FA Cup Third Round Replay 12 January 1938

The appeal of the FA Cup to a Third Division (South) team with a chance of beating a First Division club was demonstrated when Swindon managed to hold Grimsby to a draw and bring them back to the County Ground in January 1938. Only 14,000 had seen the match at Grimsby (or rather Cleethorpes, for Grimsby do not actually play in Grimsby itself). Swindon's right-winger, Jones, had given the Robins a lead after twenty-seven minutes but the Mariners struck back when their English international Bestall laid on an equaliser for Tomlinson.

For the replay the number of police at the County Ground was increased from four to seven and the club purchased two megaphones to help with crowd control. With such scant resources a crowd of 23,000 was happily managed. The match was fought out on a ground only made playable by the spreading of large quantities of sand, specially purchased from Porthcawl. Swindon lost the toss and attacked the Town End in the first half. Grimsby looked a class or two above Swindon in the opening period and it came as no surprise when Bryan could only punch out a centre to Tomlinson, who put the visitors in front.

Swindon came more into the game in the second half and Jones forced two brilliant saves from Tweedy in the Grimsby goal. Only five minutes remained when Swindon eventually got their equaliser. The goal came from Ben Morton. Morton had been Swindon's first £1,000 signing when he joined them from Torquay. It seemed a very poor investment indeed when after seventeen games he had failed to score a single goal but in this match he at last broke his Swindon duck. His goal produced the following description: 'Flat out in bogland, Grimsby's blond 'keeper saw Morton scoop the ball into the net. Colleagues hugged Morton as though he were Josephine Baker and when he fell, injured like Nelson in his hour of triumph, the crowd gave him a cheer that might have frightened the fishes up Grimsby way.' A stop-press entry in the *Advertiser* described the goal as 'having produced cheering that lasted for five minutes and was heard three miles away'.

Five minutes of extra time remained when Alan Fowler, who was later to be one of three Town players killed in the Second World War, converted a centre by left-winger Heatherington to put Swindon into the fourth round, where Luton ended the Robins' cup hopes.

Older supporters recall that a number of Commonweal pupils bunked off school to see the match and lost their prefects' badges as a result. One hopes the result made them feel the sacrifice was worthwhile.

Swindon Town: Bryan; Tonner, Smith; Cousins, Morrall, Wilcockson; Jones, Fowler, Morton, Bradley, Hetherington.
Grimsby Town: Tweedy; Vincent, Hodgson; Hall, Betmead, Buck; Dyson, Bestall, Tomlinson, Craven, Coulter.
Attendance: 23,101

Right: Jackie Bestall, one of England's many one-cap wonders and scorer of Grimsby's goal, shown on a John Sinclair Ltd cigarette card.

Below: Goalmouth action from the Grimsby tie.

Swindon Town v. Aldershot

Swindon Town 2 Aldershot 2
Football League Third Division (South) 1 September 1939

The first two games of the new season had brought no points for Swindon. Anxious to add punch to the attack, manager Neil Harris brought in John McKenzie, who had scored five in a reserve match against Bath City, in place of Ben Morton. Alan Fowler moved to outside right to replace the injured Eddie Jones, while Day came in for Ryan at left half.

Swindon were rocked by an early goal from Palmer after six minutes. It seemed another blow to their hopes was struck when, following a blow in the face, McKenzie was left with a severe nosebleed. He continued to play, but was something of a passenger, being forced to move to a wide position where he clutched a cloth to his nose. It was an extremely unfortunate piece of luck for him, as this was to be his only outing in League football. For Swindon, the injury did have a silver lining as Alan Fowler moved to the centre-forward spot. It was Fowler who got the Swindon equaliser in the thirty-fourth minute when Hedley, who was Town's most threatening forward in this game, centred for him to score with a header. Two minutes later, Fowler scored again when his long shot was fumbled by the Aldershot 'keeper to give Town the lead. Fowler, at 5ft 7in, was considered by many to be too small for a centre forward but match reporter 'NJB' noted that he was 'too good a player to be left out of the side'. Although this was his first appearance of the season, his 67 goals scored in 173 League matches for Town since joining them from Leeds indicated he was a considerable force in Third Division football.

The second half saw Aldershot obtain an equaliser through Hurst and but for some good anticipation by Frank Wildman in dashing out to the edge of his area to clear, Town might have conceded a further goal. The match report mentions that Day improved and that 'Francis and Lucas produced some clever runs, but were below last season's form.' Neil Harris was expected to have a lot more grey hairs unless there was a speedy change for the better.

The review of the match the following Monday ended with the telling sentence 'I am afraid there will be lots of changes before we next see Swindon in action.' The reason for this was the declaration of war and the resultant banning of gatherings for sport or entertainment. This had come about from the fear that bombing raids would devastate centres of population and large crowds could cause huge civilian casualties. When this did not happen and the 'phoney war' period developed, the government relented and a South-West Regional League was formed in which Swindon finished a creditable fifth, with Alan Fowler top scorer with 18 goals. Of the Swindon team in this match, three – Fowler, Imrie and Olney – would perish in the Second World War and only two – Parkhouse, who made a single appearance, and Billy Lucas – would play when the Football League proper was restored in 1946/47 season.

Swindon Town: Wildman; Parkhouse, Lowe; Imrie Olney, Day; Fowler, Francis, McKenzie, Lucas, Hedley.
Aldershot: Greaves; Eastwood, Kelly; Palmer, Summerbee, Clark; Proud, Chalmers, Ray, Dawes, Hurst.

The wording on the plaque which can be seen in the club foyer commemorating three players who perished serving their country in the Second World War.

SWINDON TOWN v. WATFORD

Swindon Town 5 Watford 0
Football League Third Division (South) 11 January 1947

The requisitioning of the County Ground had meant the war had caused even more disruption to Swindon than many of their fellow teams. Life in Swindon was getting back to normal, however, and while nationally the road haulage strike was causing concern, on the local front people could look forward to the pantomime *Mother Goose* at the Empire and view plans for a magnificent new hotel to be built (although it never was) at the Swindon Junction railway station. January 1947 was to see the appearance on the footballing scene of someone whose time at Swindon would outlast the Empire Theatre and do more to enhance the Town's reputation in the years that followed.

Maurice Owen had fought with the Chindits in Burma and already made an impact on Swindon with 8 goals in 3 reserve matches. Hence, when Bill Stephens was ordered to take a complete rest Louis Page, the Town manager, had no hesitation in plunging the youngster from Abingdon into his team. It was certainly not a settled team which he stepped into to make his debut. The local press were concerned that twenty-two players had already been used by Swindon. Maurice was not the only player to make his debut that day. An injury to Don Emery meant that Dick Parkhouse was brought into the side at right-back, with Albert Young, who had recovered from a thigh injury, switching to left-back. Only two Town players had been ever-present during the season, these being the skipper, Welsh international Billy Lucas, and Billy Lloyd. The impact of the County Ground being used as a prisoner-of-war camp compounded by the bad winter had combined to leave the pitch a quagmire and the mud slopped around the players' ankles as they ran on to the pitch. Owen made an immediate impact not as scorer but as creator, setting up Slacker Williams who was able to shoot Town into the lead in the third minute. 'RCE', the *Advertiser* reporter, was fulsome in his praise of the newcomer in Town's forward line. 'Give it to Maurice' was the headline over an article which went on to describe how he had stayed in the centre, got up well to high balls and how his shooting had been both accurate and dangerous. With half an hour gone, Maurice scored the first of his 166 goals for Town, shooting in from distance.

Watford came into the game more in the second half, but seldom looked like unsettling the Town defence. If some clearances by Parkhouse were sliced, Young seldom wasted a ball, while Jimmy Ithell at centre half was a tower of strength, as was Eddie Painter who did well to blot out Young, the Watford schemer. Three more Town goals came in the last twenty minutes, the first from Williams and then two more from Owen. By the season's end, Owen had notched 13 more goals, way behind Stephens, the man whom he had come into the team to replace, who scored 26 league goals that year (a figure still not exceeded for Swindon in post-war football) and who was moved to a right-wing berth on his return to fitness. Swindon finished in a highly creditable fourth position and could look forward to the future with confidence.

Swindon Town: Boulton; Parkhouse, Young; Lloyd, Ithell, Painter; E.M. Jones, Lucas, Owen, Paterson, Williams.
Watford: Chase; Drinkwater, Evans; Farner, Gillespie, Harper; Harris, Morgan, Thompson, Wipfler, Young.
Attendance: 34,229
Gate receipts: £1,042 4s 7d

AGAINST WATFORD ON SATURDAY —

"SLACKER" WILLIAMS NETTED OUR FIRST GOAL AFTER 3 MINUTES, WITH MAURICE OWEN IN CLOSE ATTENDANCE

ONE MORE FROM "SLACKER" & TWO MORE FROM MAURICE BROUGHT SWINDON'S TOTAL TO 5

30 MINUTES LATER OWEN SCORED HIS FIRST GOAL FOR THE TOWN TEAM

& THE FINAL SCORE TO 5-0! (THANKS TO SOME EXCELLENT MUD BATH DEFENDING BY FRANK BOULTON)

THE BALL — TOOK A WICKED DELIGHT IN THE MUD!

11-1-47

Above: An *Evening Advertiser* cartoon summarising the match that was Maurice Owen's debut.

Left: Maurice Owen built on his success in this match, scoring 16 goals in his first 17 matches, including four in one match against Mansfield. He was to set a new record of 601 for club appearances.

BURNLEY v. SWINDON TOWN

Burnley 0 Swindon Town 2
FA Cup Third Round 10 January 1948

During the twentieth century, no side had managed to complete the League and Cup double until Tottenham achieved this feat in the sixties. A club that went very close, finishing as both runners-up in the League and defeated FA Cup finalists, was Burnley in 1947. Given this, it was a mammoth task Swindon faced the following season when the third-round draw forced them to travel to Turf Moor. The bookies obviously fancied a Burnley win, as odds as short as 10-1 could be obtained on the Lancashire side to win the Cup while Swindon were priced at 5,000-1. Swindon had reached the third round with victories over Ipswich and Aldershot in a tie which had taken a second match to decide. Swindon travelled to Southport for pre-match training that was fairly traditional for the period, consisting of golf, walks and a visit to the brine baths. The South-West Regional Commission for Transport, which had to approve travel and fuel consumption, reversed its original decision not to allow coaches to run to Burnley, but by that time it was too late for coach companies to change their plans and most Swindon fans had to be content to listen to progress reports that were broadcast at the County Ground during the reserve match with Bristol Rovers, and hope that Portsmouth manager Jack Tinn's lucky cup spats, lent to Town for this match, would work their magic.

At this time, requests were made to the FA to bring kick-offs forward in case bad light prohibited the match being played to a conclusion. Surprisingly, at a time when extra time was being played in the first match of a tie to reduce travel, these were rejected, even though the measure would have saved the extra travelling costs incurred when matches were not decided at the first attempt. Many felt Swindon's best hope was to try to hang on for a draw and hope for a curtailment of extra time that would at least generate another gate at the County Ground. Town's manager, Louis Page, himself a former Burnley player, adopted a more positive strategy. He went to watch Burnley play Bolton the previous week and used this to devise tactics that he declined to share before the match but spoke of afterwards. Summed up, they were 'to play football and beat Burnley to the punch'. He had programmed his team to watch out for the prevalence of Burnley attacks coming from the left. He had noted how Burnley's wing halves would throw the ball to inside men who would lay it back to full-backs who were left unopposed. Town's wingers pushed up to stop this and also made sure that Knight, the Burnley schemer, was harassed as soon as he got near the ball. Perhaps most crucial of all, Maurice Owen was instructed to drop deep. This prevented him becoming an isolated figure and enabled him to run at the Burnley defence. This tactic produced an early dividend when Morris Jones passed to him and he ran forward and beat centre half Brown before laying the ball off to Dryden, who scored with a flashing low cross-shot. The game was only two minutes old but this was a key boost to the 'railwaymen' as the Burnley press labelled them. 'RCE' described Swindon as 'a side with more craftsmanship, with more enterprise and with unquenchable enthusiasm and team spirit.' Five minutes before half-time, Town increased their lead. Strong in the Burnley goal raced out to collect a through ball and appeared to just beat Owen to it. The Town number nine managed to dislodge the ball from the grip of the diving 'keeper but in so doing was left flat out. He managed to perform a contortionist act, however, and succeeded in sticking out a leg and hooking the ball into the empty goal.

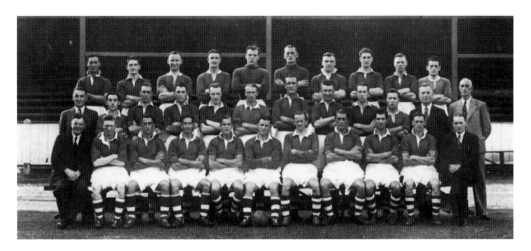

Above: The Swindon squad for 1947/48 in a pre-season line-up.

Right: Maurice Owen, scorer of Swindon's second goal.

The opening twenty minutes of the second half saw Town coming under heavy pressure, but they managed to hold out. Perhaps the key moment came when Burnley were awarded a penalty. The kick was taken by Harry Potts, later to become Burnley manager. The kick was not the best and Frank Boulton, who had been sound throughout, managed to get down and smother it. A goal at this stage could well have sparked a revival from the First Division side but as time wore on Swindon's stamina helped them wrest the initiative back from Burnley. It had been very much a team effort but captain Billy Lucas, 'a tireless example to his men', and Jimmy Ithell stopped up the middle to such good effect that the former Bristol City man Billingham was moved to try his luck at centre forward but to no avail. A crowd of around 3,000 awaited the team on their return to Swindon, although only five of the team were actually on the train that reached Swindon station to receive the congratulations of Deputy Mayor Alderman Selman.

Burnley: Strong; Woodruff, Mather; Attwell, Brown, Bray; Billingham, Potts, Harrison, J. Knight, Hays.
Swindon Town: Boulton; Young, Emery; Kaye, Ithell, Painter; Dryden, Lucas, Owen, Jones, Maguire.
Attendance: 34,229

STOKE CITY V. SWINDON TOWN

Stoke City 0 Swindon Town 1
FA Cup Fourth Round Replay 4 February 1952

The first match at the County Ground had attracted a big crowd, with the queue beginning to form at 7.30 a.m. A Mrs Violet Carter was first in line, explaining that she wanted to ensure a good spot on Stratton Bank. She was to see Swindon get a flying start when a centre from Betteridge was met by Jimmy Bain, who swivelled and shot into the City goal. City pegged Swindon back with an equaliser a minute after the start of the second half and with Swindon not at their best it was generally reckoned that Swindon were a mite fortunate to earn a replay.

For some reason this took place in double quick time. The original match at the County Ground was played on the Saturday and the replay was just two days later on the Monday. Some 300 Town fans followed their team to the Potteries. One of them was Frank Harvey. He seems to have been a touch clairvoyant. An employee of British Rail, he had been so confident of Town forcing a draw that he had a booked a day off work the previous week to ensure he could go to the replay. 'We will probably lose but I hope we win' was the sentiment expressed by many of the Robins' fans. Perhaps their hopes rose a little when they saw the state of the pitch. Despite the attention of a dozen men who had spent the day breaking ice and scattering salt it was described by the *Advertiser's* correspondent as 'more fit for duck shooting than a football match' and many were surprised that referee Mr Williams of Nottingham allowed the match to proceed. As in the match at Swindon, the Town were in blue shirts, something which had caused problems for the rosette sellers who had been hawking red favours for Swindon on the Saturday, while Stoke wore white. Stoke dominated the opening ten minutes. Three attacks down the left came to nothing but when Sellars controlled the ball well and got in a shot it flew inches wide of Norman Uprichard's post. After this, Swindon came into the game. Two centres by Bain unsettled the Stoke defence and when Owen

The Swindon squad that took Swindon to the fifth round of the cup.

George 'Garth' Hudson who proved a pillar of strength at the heart of Town's defence.

(who was roving about the forward line to pull Mountford out of position) centred Lunn was left with a golden opportunity which he blazed wide. Swindon's players were combining well and looked certain to score when Millar raced through only to be pulled back by the linesman's flag. Harry Lunn twice went close for Swindon, heading just over the bar and then grazing the crossbar with a free-kick from just outside the area. The goal Swindon's play deserved came when Herod was stranded out of his goal. The ball broke to Millar just outside the corner of the penalty box. Sizing up the situation, the Scotsman struck a shot from the edge of the area, which defeated a desperate attempt by Martin to race back and clear.

The second half saw Maurice Owen come into his element. In the first game, he had been strangely quiet, but now Mountford had his work cut out to contain the Town star. He nearly increased Town's lead when he got the ball out of Herod's grasp, only for it to squirm away from

Stoke City v. Swindon Town

Harry Lunn twice went close for Swindon.

him along the goal line. He missed out again when he raced to fire the ball into an empty net only to lose his footing on the treacherous surface. His magnificent efforts were all the more remarkable in the light of the fact that at the game's end when he removed one of his boots, which had lost part of the toe cap, the nail of a stud had pressed through the sole and cut into his foot. The final fifteen minutes saw a desperate assault by the Potters. Superlatives litter the report of the Town's defence at this stage. May on the left was 'brilliant' Hunt was 'the complete full-back' while George Hudson was said to have 'won absolutely everything in the penalty area'.

Stoke City: Herod; Mould, McCue; Martin, Mountfield, Kirton; Malkin, Bowyer, Sellars, Smyth, Oscroft.
Swindon Town: Uprichard; Hunt, May; Kay, Hudson, Gray; Lunn, Millar, Owen, Betteridge, Bain.
Attendance: 29,332

SWINDON TOWN v. READING

Swindon Town 2 Reading 0
Football League Third Division (South), 4 May 1955

The penultimate game of the season 1954/55 was a local derby with the added spice that if Swindon could win they would avoid having to apply for re-election for the first time since the Second World War. Swindon's line-up showed one change from the side that had beaten Coventry 3-0 and drawn 0-0 with Torquay in consecutive home games. The change was at outside left where Mickey Bull came in for Alex Hope.

The first attempt on goal came from Henry Williams, one of five players in the Swindon team who had already been placed on the transfer list, when he blazed over from a free-kick. He enjoyed better fortune after a shot by Riseborough broke to him and he found the net with a good shot from outside the area. Ray Sampson fired two long shots over the bar before Reading retaliated with Uphill putting in an effort that skimmed Burton's crossbar. An injury to Reading 'keeper Jones forced him to hand the green jersey to his colleague Reeves and to spend the rest of the match as an outfield player. Cyril Riseborough seems to have been the pick of the Swindon players in the first half. In the first of his three seasons with Swindon, the Doncaster-born player impressed with some good distribution of the ball. Reading pressed forwards towards the end of the half but their shots were from long range and inaccurate, so the Town goal did not seem in danger.

Four minutes into the second half, Reading might have equalised but Sam Burton made a fine save from an effort by Campbell following a corner. Riseborough beat Mansell and set up Sampson for a shot. This was pulled down by stand-in 'keeper Reeves but bounced awkwardly and just went over the goal line to give Town a 2-0 lead. Although local lad Sampson remained on the Town books for three more seasons this was to prove his last goal in first-team football. It could hardly have come at a better time, for after it Swindon were rarely on the offensive and as Reading pressed forward the two-goal cushion helped to calm a few nerves. A Dixon shot was deflected for a corner and George Hunt needed to clear off his line with Burton beaten as the Biscuits poured forward. Henry Williams might have scored for Town in a breakaway but the pressure was soon back on the Town goal. Burton did well to cut out a hard driven cross by Hinshelwood and Wheeler should have scored when he hit a shot straight at the Town 'keeper, who held it well.

It was to prove a timely victory, for Swindon collected no points from their last match, a 7-0 defeat at Shrewsbury, but remained ahead of Exeter who drew their final game, while Walsall and Colchester had to re-apply for League status. Perhaps it was just as well, for Swindon finished in the bottom two spots in the following two seasons and three consecutive applications for re-election might have tested even the old boy network.

Swindon Town: Burton; Hunt, Hilton; Batchelor, Hudson, G. Williams; Riseborough, Sampson, R. Onslow, H. Williams, Ball.
Reading: Jones; Pensford, Mansell; Campbell, Reeves, McLaren; Hinshelwood, Uphill, Dixon, Leach, Wheeler.
Attendance: 5,147

Sam Burton, who pulled off several fine saves in the victory over Reading.

SWINDON TOWN v. NORWICH CITY

Swindon Town 1 Norwich City 1
FA Cup Second Round 6 December 1958

Saturday 6 December 1958 – Matt Busby had just resigned as manager of Scotland on doctor's orders and Swindon Boys had fought their way to the divisional final of the English Schools' Shield. It was the second round of the FA Cup and a day that saw Tooting & Mitcham defeat Northampton Town 2-1 and Peterborough defeat Headington United 4-2 in a cream-of-the-non-Leaguers clash.

Swindon faced a home match with Norwich, one of the best-supported teams in the Third Division with gates averaging over 22,000. Jim Kelly, recovered from a shin injury, led the Swindon forwards while Nethercott in goal and Terry Allcock at inside right returned to the Norwich team. Swindon had much the better of the first half and took the lead after twenty minutes. Bob Edwards stabbed a pass out to Willie Corbett, whose centre was headed in by John Richards. Jimmy Hill, picked out by 'RCE' as the best forward on the pitch, equalised for City after thirty-eight minutes. The goal came after Errol Crossan rounded Town full-back Walter Bingley and cut in along the by-line before pulling the ball back to allow Hill to score. Swindon came close to restoring their lead just before the interval but Nethercott did well to keep out an Edwards' piledriver.

The second half saw Norwich gradually gain the ascendancy, with big Barry Butler stamping out Swindon's attacks and Archie Macauley's team building some clever passing movements. They might have snatched victory in the final minute when Allcock broke through, but he was unable to beat Sam Burton in the Swindon goal.

By the time the replay was staged both sides knew that a home tie with Manchester United was the reward for victory. Kelly, who had appeared to tire in the first match, was replaced by Maurice Owen, who played in a deep-lying centre-forward role with the inside forwards pushed further forward in the fashion of the Hungarians. A penalty appeal for Norwich, when the ball struck Jack Fountain, was turned down. Near the end of the half, they again went close but Burton managed to snatch a fierce effort by Roy McCrohan from under the bar.

The second half saw Nethercott forced to leave the field shortly after he had rescued his side by diving at the feet of Edwards. Matt Crowe replaced him for a few minutes but soon after their 'keeper's return the Canaries struck, Crossan scoring with a powerful drive which Burton could not get enough of a hand on to divert wide. Swindon piled forward after this and Corbett and Morgan both tested the City 'keeper while big George Hudson came forward to add his height to the attack. However, it was to no avail and it was Norwich who had the opportunity to face United in the third round. It was a chance they took with both hands. Not only did they defeat them, they also beat Cardiff City, Tottenham and Sheffield United. Their bid to become the first Third Division side at Wembley failed at the final hurdle, against Luton Town in the semi-final.

Swindon Town: Burton; Neal, Bingley (Lee); Morgan, Hudson, Owen (Fountain); Corbett, Richards, Kelly (Owen), Edwards, Darcy.

Norwich City: Nethercott; Thurlow, Ashman; McCrohan, Butler, Crowe; Crossan, Alcock, Bly (Clelland), Hill, Brennan.

Names in brackets below refer to changes to teams in the replay.

Attendance: 14,755 (replay 12,235)

SWINDON TOWN v. NORWICH CITY

Above: The centre spread of a programme showing a host of local advertisers. The final score and the Norwich scorer have been marked in but Richards has not been noted as the Town scorer.

Left: Town left-winger Arnold Darcy, whose first-round hat-trick set up the tie with Norwich.

BATH CITY v. SWINDON TOWN

Bath City 4 Swindon Town 6
FA Cup First Round Replay 10 November 1960

After conceding goals in the ninth and eleventh minutes of their FA Cup first-round match with Bath City at the County Ground, Swindon's hopes of progressing in the competition looked slim. Two goals in the second half gave them a chance to survive, although with home advantage gone against a side that had put out both Millwall and Notts County in progressing to the third round the previous season, hopes were not high. The Town manager, Bert Head, pinned his hopes on the fact that the heavy conditions in the first match had not helped his young side and on a better surface they might yet prevail.

Swindon made one change, bringing in Crooks for Sam Burton, who was struggling with a shoulder injury. Rain began to fall as the game started but did little to spoil a classic cup tie with play switching from end to end. First blood was drawn by Swindon when Ernie Hunt set up David 'Bronco' Layne to score in the eleventh minute. Then Bath City's Scottish international Charlie 'Cannonball' Fleming latched onto the ball in a goalmouth scrimmage and evaded two tackles before slotting the ball home in the twenty-seventh minute. Three minutes before half-time a piledriver of a free-kick by Layne gave Town a 2-1 lead at the interval.

Swindon increased their lead in the forty-eighth minute when Ernie Hunt turned on a pass from Keith Morgan and gave Black in the City goal no chance. Swindon must have thought they had the game won when Hunt scored again, prodding the ball home after a corner. A misjudgement by Crook saw a free-kick by Tony Book, later to earn fame with Manchester City, sail over the 'keeper's head into the net. Such greasy conditions were not easy for 'keepers and a fumble by the former Scottish international goalkeeper Black at the other end allowed Layne to complete his hat-trick. Within two minutes, first Fleming and then O'Neil scored for Bath and a seemingly impregnable 5-2 lead had shrunk to a single goal and looked distinctly insecure. Eight minutes from time, Layne headed his fourth goal to calm the nerves of Swindon fans in the crowd of 12,818. Surprisingly in such a high-scoring match, 'RCE' in his report singled out defender Maurice Owen for the highest praise, particularly in the early stages when his anticipation and tackling had held Bath at bay. Town's victory meant a second-round home tie against Shrewsbury, which the Robins lost 1-0.

Nine of the team which featured in this cup tie stayed together into the 1962/63 season when Town won their first ever Football League promotion. The odd men out were 'Bronco' Layne, whose career was to end in disgrace when he was jailed for match fixing when playing for Sheffield Wednesday, and Crooks, whose one first-team appearance this was. Even more remarkably, eight of the nine were home-grown talent, the odd man out being Arnold Darcy, who was signed from Wigan.

Bath City: Black; Hale, Book; Skuse, Scott, Meadows; Fletcher, Fleming, Wiltshire, O'Neil, Thomas.
Swindon Town: Crook; Wollen, Trollope; Morgan, Owen, Woodruff; Summerbee, Hunt, Layne, Jackson, Darcy.
Attendance: 12,818

Above: The cover of the match programme.

Left: Tony Book, shown here on a *Sun* swap card, was a member of the Bath City team and went on to win League and cup honours with Manchester City.

SWINDON TOWN v. QUEENS PARK RANGERS

Swindon Town 5 Queens Park Rangers 0
Football League Third Division 12 January 1963

With the country in the icy grip of one of the worst winters people could remember, a record forty-two out of the forty-six matches that made up the League fixture list were called off. One of the four to survive was at the County Ground. Seventeen inches of snow had been cleared from the pitch and was piled up in four-foot-high walls around the playing pitch. A quarter-inch covering of snow had been left to insulate the surface and mixed with sand. Referee Mr Hough made a midday inspection and declared the ground fit. 'An old soldier is a cautious soldier' was the explanation given when the 8th Army that had made such speedy advances became bogged down in the Bocage country of Normandy. There may have been something of this in the reason why Swindon seemed happier to play than the much more experienced Rangers, whose manager, Alec Stock, made a formal protest about the match being allowed to proceed.

Swindon's side showed two changes from the previous match, with Mike Turner and Cliff Jackson both having recovered from leg injuries to reclaim their first-team spots. As the game got underway it did seem that Swindon were adapting better to the conditions than the Londoners, but this may well have been due to the footwear of Bata basketball boots that the Town players were wearing. Sensibly, in the cold conditions, the Swindon players also took to wearing yellow gloves. Drinkwater was the busier of the two 'keepers, but it was Mike Turner who had to receive attention after a courageous double save. First he had pushed out a shot from McClelland, before scrambling up quickly to block an effort by Mark Lazarus close in on goal. The first goal did not come until twenty-nine minutes had elapsed. Summerbee chased a ball down the right and just managed to catch it before it went out of play. He quickly screwed it back across goal where the inrushing Town player Jack Smith slid in on one knee to score. Just before half-time, Smith nearly added a second with a header, but Drinkwater produced a fine diving save.

Four minutes into the second half, the floodlights were switched on, producing a strange contrast between the floodlit white snow and the dark beneath the stands and on the terraces. Drinkwater made a courageous save and two Swindon corners followed, with the second seeing Angell having to head out from under his own bar. Two further corners for Swindon produced no opportunity, but a clever free-kick by Bobby Woodruff saw Drinkwater just getting back to tip over the bar. When Rangers got a corner, Lazarus curled it dangerously close to the Swindon goal but Mike Turner rose to hold it well. In the sixty-second minute Swindon scored their second. A free-kick by McPherson was gathered by Don Rogers in the Rangers area and he neatly nipped between the defenders to shoot home. Hunt had a goal disallowed for offside before Swindon scored their third in the eighty-first minute. Although Swindon dominated the game it is worth noting that the last three goals came in the final ten minutes of the match, two in the last three. It was perhaps at this stage, with the game lost, that Rangers saw the sustaining of an injury in an already lost cause as foolish and so contributed to the one-sided scoreline. Smith completed his hat-trick, first shooting past the already grounded Drinkwater, and then getting the ball in from close range.

Should the game have been played? Stan Halsey of the *Sunday Pictorial* thought not: 'In my view, Alec Stock was right. It was a glacier of a pitch.' The BBC's Brian Butler agreed with him. Max Marquis of *The Times*, however, felt 'the game was surprisingly better than one could expect'.

SWINDON TOWN v. QUEENS PARK RANGERS

John Smith opens the scoring for Town on a snowbound County Ground.

Responding to accusations of doctoring the pitch, Bert Head declared he had not done anything 'except my duty to club and public to get a pitch ready'. It is perhaps interesting that, although the pitch got a little icy towards the end, for much of the game it made for more flowing football than the heavy mud that often provided a surface at the County Ground in this period. The only casualties were a number of Swindon players who developed boils, seemingly caused by the sand, and the relationship between Bert Head and Alec Stock. Previously good friends, for a period they became involved in a bitter slanging match in press cuttings that followed the game.

Swindon Town: Turner; Owen, Trollope; Morgan, McPherson, Woodruff; Summerbee, Hunt, Smith, Jackson, Rogers.

Queens Park Rangers: Drinkwater; Ingham, Angell; Large, Keen, Malcolm; Lazarus, Barber, Leary, Bedford, McClelland.

Attendance 7,450

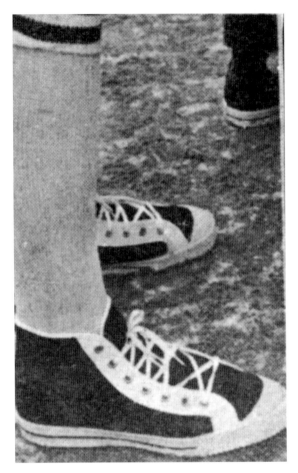

Above: The basketball boots that proved Swindon's secret weapon.

Right: Bata were not slow to cash in on Swindon's success.

Swindon Town v. Bristol City

Swindon Town 3 Bristol City 2
Football League Third Division 2 March 1963

I have included this match as it was really the game in which Bert Head's 'babes' came of age. They had already shown they could play quality football but in this game they showed they could stand up to a physically more powerful side even when they had experienced setbacks. In the week before the match, a rumour was circulating that Bert Head had been offered the manager's position at Brighton but had said, 'We are seeing the results of five years' hard graft. I want to see it through to the end.' This match showed just how much Bert had achieved in his five years at the club and marked out Town as real promotion contenders.

Keith Morgan won the toss and as was traditional at this time elected to attack the Stratton Bank goal in the first half, so that Town could kick towards their own most vocal supporters in the Town End during the second half. The pitch under the Shrivenham Road stand was hard and slippery but the rest of the pitch began to cut up once the game got underway. Driven forward by wing halves Keith Morgan and Bobby Woodruff, the Town forwards were prominent in the early stages and Cliff Jackson might have done better in the sixth minute when he stubbed his kick when well placed. The most dangerous City forward during this period was Tate and he sent over an excellent cross which former England centre forward Johnny Atyeo only just failed to reach when the goal would have been at his mercy. An international of the future was also prominent in the action, namely Mike Summerbee, who made some strong runs down the right and one solid shot that was not quite straight enough. Then came a period when Mike O'Hara's goalkeeping might have got Town in trouble. Firstly, he failed to reach a cross from the dangerous Tait and was left stranded, but, fortunately for Swindon, Ken McPherson was well placed to head clear. Then, secondly, O'Hara was beaten again minutes later by a shot from Johnny Atyeo but his shot struck the foot of the post. In the thirty-first minute a corner was headed clear by the blond head of Bobby Woodruff only to fall to Briggs who had O'Hara diving desperately to save. In the thirty-fifth minute City took a deserved lead when Williams shot from the left side of the goal. O'Hara appeared to have the ball covered but unfortunately it found the net via the Australian's shoulder. Four minutes from half-time City had a lucky escape, when Hunt neatly headed a strong shot by Woodruff on to the target only for it to strike a City defender on the chest.

The second half started disastrously for Swindon with a long ball from Connor being headed down by Atyeo to Clark, who drove it home. 'Good football even if it cost points' had been Bert Head's cry at Ashton Gate earlier in the season when City had muscled Swindon out of a two-goal lead. Now it was Swindon's turn to come back. The start of the fightback had a shade of fortune about it with Thresher and Jack Smith running for a ball together and the City man appearing to get his legs tangled with the Town centre forward. Referee Pickles pointed to the spot and, as he was to do on the six other occasions during the season when he was called on to take a penalty, Ernie Hunt made no mistake. With twenty-five minutes remaining, Swindon equalised. Again, it was a shade fortunate but if you keep the ball in your opponents' half, as Swindon did for much of the time, breaks will come. Keith Morgan had seen his shot blocked and Summerbee fired in the rebound that seemed to take a slight deflection on its way into the goal. Swindon pressed forward after this but, as time grew short, the play became more even and it appeared Town would have to settle for a point. However, in the

Above: A team photograph featuring Ernie Hunt, whose displays during this season were to help him gain international recognition. From left to right, back row: Summerbee, Woodruff, Trollope, Dawson, Atkins, Morgan, Turner, McPherson, Smith, Owen. Front row: Huxford, Darcy, Hunt, Harber, Cousins (trainer), O'Hara, Stevens, Smart, Darcy, Jackson.

Right: John Atyeo, an England international who starred for City but after his retirement became a regular spectator at the County Ground.

eightieth minute, Smith broke into the box and went down under pressure. The referee consulted a linesman and when he awarded an indirect free-kick, rather than a penalty, many Swindon fans were disappointed. The disappointment was to be short-lived, with Smith reacting quickly to a powerful shot from Hunt, hooking the ball into the goal and so giving Town a win which took Swindon to the top of the Third Division table, ahead of Peterborough on goal average.

Swindon Town: O'Hara; Dawson, Trollope; Morgan, McPherson, Woodruff; Summerbee, Hunt, Smith, Jackson, Darcy.
Bristol City: Nicholls; Briggs, Thresher; Parr, Connor, Etheridge; Tait, Clark, Atyeo, Williams, Derrick.
Attendance: 16,778

SWINDON TOWN v. SHREWSBURY TOWN

Swindon Town 1 Shrewsbury Town 0
Football League Third Division 14 May 1963

When Keith Morgan led his team out onto a muddy and slippery County Ground pitch, Second Division football was within Swindon's grasp after forty years of trying. Shrewsbury were in a safe position with nothing to play for and all Swindon needed to do was to repeat the victory they had achieved at Gay Meadow earlier in the season to ensure Second Division football would come to the County Ground for the first time.

Swindon did not open well. Passes went astray and Bert Head was to explain this as 'acute tension which badly disrupted our play tonight'. In contrast, Shrewsbury played some good football but their attack, possibly due to the absence of veteran striker Arthur Rowley, lacked a cutting edge. Graham French, who was to be signed by Swindon the following season, made a clever run but it ended with a shot across goal that went wide of the far post. Middleton tried three or four long shots for the 'Shrews' but none really troubled Mike Turner. It was his opposite number, Miller, who was at the centre of perhaps the most exciting incident of the first half. Advancing from his goal he just managed to knock the ball away from Ernie Hunt only for it to fall into the path of the advancing Mike Summberbee. Agilely the 'keeper threw himself down and blocked the shot. A corner by Summerbee was headed goalward by Roger Smart, but again Miller produced a fine save. It was by no means one-way traffic though, and at the other end it required Turner to dive under the feet of Middleton to prevent the visitors taking the lead. Just before half-time the crowd erupted when Ernie Hunt drilled the ball into the net, but the celebrations were short-lived as the raised flag of the linesman was spotted.

Early in the second half Town had an incredible escape. Napoleon used to ask of his generals: 'Never mind if he's very good, is he lucky?' Mike Turner would certainly have won his approval, for it often seemed luck when the 'keeper Town had bought out of the RAF stopped shots with his feet. A shot by Gregson had struck Turner's foot but still looked goal-bound when Town full-back Owen Dawson pulled out 'a most amazing and valuable interception' getting the ball away from virtually under the crossbar. Play switched to the other end and an appeal for hands against Pountney was turned down by Mr Stokes the referee, who must have felt that the ball played the man. Bert Head had always put his faith in youth, never more so than before the previous game at Colchester, when he had called up a left-wing partnership of Roger Smart and Cliff Jackson to replace Bill Atkins and Arnold Darcy. Smart had repaid him with the two goals that brought victory and now he was to score another priceless goal. John Stevens, another man with an RAF background, knocked the ball away from Miller on the left-hand side of goal. Smart stabbed a long shot goalwards. For what seemed an eternity the ball rolled towards goal as Miller chased back after it. With a last desperate dive the 'keeper caught it on the line but failed to stop it, as the ball's forward momentum carried it over the line into the Town End goal. Smart leaping high, the final whistle, the crowd on the pitch – everything seemed to happen at once. In his hour of triumph Bert Head said 'I have always been confident, right from the early stages that our youth policy would see us to the Second Division.' It was good to see that on the day following the match, a tribute was paid to Fred Coleman, the Swindon Boys' manager who had helped so many of Bert's Babes in the early years.

Swindon Town v. Shrewsbury Town

Some of the 20,000 crowd which saw Swindon Town win promotion by beating Shrewsbury Town 1—0 at the County Ground last night.

An expectant crowd before the kick-off of the Shrewsbury Town match which was to see Swindon win promotion for the first time in their history.

Swindon Town: Turner; Dawson, Trollope; Morgan, McPherson, Woodruff; Summerbee, Hunt, Stevens, Smart, Jackson.

Shrewsbury Town: Miller; Walters, Skeech; Harley, Dolby, Pountney; Gregson, Middleton, Clarke, Nixon, French.

Attendance: 20,273

Swindon Town v. Chelsea

Swindon Town 3 Chelsea 0
Football League Cup Second Round 24 September 1963

The previous Saturday a 1-0 victory over Sunderland had taken newly promoted Swindon to the top of the Second Division table. Now they faced the challenge from a side in the division above them that had, like Swindon, made youth the bedrock of their team policy. By the standards of the time, the crowd of less than 17,000 was a disappointing one, as the previous two home matches had seen crowds of over 26,000 and 28,000. Some blamed the fact that people had either been locked out at these matches or been unable to see very well and many feared Swindon would be forced to develop their facilities at the cost of strengthening the team. The presence of Stan Cullis, the manager of Wolves in the crowd, indicated that if Swindon decided to sell some of their starlets to fund ground improvements there would be no lack of buyers.

The first half belonged very much to Chelsea. Frank Blunstone tested Mike Turner in the Swindon goal with a shot from a wide angle while Dennis Brown, later to become a Swindon player himself, beat the Swindon 'keeper only to see his shot evade the far post. Swindon's goal had an even closer escape when John O'Rourke beat Turner only to see Town's veteran centre half Ken McPherson clear the shot off the line. The half-time corner count of eight to three in favour of Chelsea was a fair indication of the balance of the play.

The half-time interval saw Bert Head calling on his players to close the Chelsea players down more quickly. Probably in the footballing parlance of today it would have been said that Swindon had paid their opponents too much respect. Perhaps, doubting their own capacity, Town had

Ron 'Chopper' Harris played for Chelsea in this match and later became owner of a golf course at Shrivenham.

Queues like this to buy tickets for cup matches at the County Ground were not unusual in the early sixties. The back of the now-demolished old stand, bought from the Aldershot Military Tattoo ground in the late fifties, can be seen in the background.

appeared cautious and hesitant and allowed themselves to be pushed onto the defensive for much of the game. The second half saw them take the game to the visitors and they experienced the stroke of fortune that often comes the way of a team that pushes forward and chances a few speculative shots. Roger Smart tried his luck from twenty-five yards and although he struck it well it would probably not have caused a 'keeper of Peter Bonetti's quality much trouble had it not clipped the shoulder of Alan Harris and veered out of his reach. This goal came with the second half four minutes old and put Swindon in the driving seat. They tightened their grip on the game in the seventy-first minute when a scramble developed in the Chelsea goalmouth. Bonetti was mixed up in the tangle of bodies and when the ball broke loose, Jack Smith calmly slotted it through a narrow gap into the net. Three minutes later Smith scored an even more spectacular goal, turning on the spot to hit a long-range volley which arced over Bonetti and dipped into the net. Marvin Hinton, making his Chelsea debut after signing for £35,000 from Charlton, was thrown into attack in a forlorn bid by the Londoners to retrieve the game, but it was too late by far. The next morning, with their team sitting on top of the Second Division with 16 points out of a possible 18 and having just removed a First Division side from the cup, well might Swindon fans reflect that, as was said of the French Revolution, 'bliss was it in that dawn to be alive, but to be young was very heaven.'

Swindon Town: Turner; Dawson, Trollope; Morgan, McPherson, Woodruff; Summerbee, Hunt, Smith, Smart, Rogers.

Chelsea: Bonetti; A. Harris, McCreadie; Hollins, Hinton, R. Harris; Brown Tambling, O'Rourke, Harmer, Blunstone.

Attendance: 17,916

Swindon Town Youth
v. Manchester United Youth

Swindon Town Youth 1 Manchester United Youth 1
FA Youth Cup Final First Leg, 27 April 1964

What strikes one most when looking at the Swindon Youth team was that this was the first and, at the time of writing, only Swindon side to reach the FA Youth Cup final, and even more significantly how much the club relied on recruiting players from the local area. Apart from Brian Foscolo, who had signed from Queens Park Rangers, and his fellow Welshman, Bernard Griffin, who came from the Merthyr area, all the other players were found locally. Tony Hicks, Denis Peapell and Richard Plumb had all appeared in the Swindon schoolboy team. Others came from Salisbury (Terry Ling), Bath (Roger Brown), Tetbury (Denis Prosser) and Kintbury (Bruce Walker). Like the great Maurice Owen, Richard Tabor came from Abingdon and, last but not least, Don Rogers originated from the Somerset coalfield area around Midsomer Norton. Their final opponents could hardly have been tougher. Manchester United had won the FA Youth Cup the first five times it was held and the wide and effective scouting system set up by Matt Busby was renowned throughout the soccer world. The competition was played on a regional basis with Swindon's toughest test having been Arsenal, who they defeated 2-0 in the fifth round, which they followed up with a 6-1 aggregate victory over Queens Park Rangers.

It was Manchester United who looked more dangerous in the opening forays and it was John Aston who had an early chance to put United in front, only to shoot wide of an open goal. Play soon swung to the other end and twice Rogers had the United defence in difficulty. Tony Hicks, who was undoubtedly Town's man of the match, had to pull off good saves from Best and Sadler. The first half hour was a relatively even contest but, after thirty-one minutes, Swindon opened the scoring. Bruce Walker showed a good turn of pace before releasing the ball with a cross-field pass to Rogers. Already an established first-teamer, Rogers beat Duff for pace before firing a low shot past Jimmy Rimmer. Close to half-time, Busby's Babes might have scored on three occasions but Hicks first kept out a shot from Albert Kinsey, then a header from George Best and, finally, smothered the ball after David Sadler had broken through.

The spectators gave Hicks warm applause as he returned to his position after the interval, but the Swindon 'keeper was no more than a spectator himself when Sadler's shot struck the bar. Manchester piled on the pressure, but could not get the ball past Tony Hicks. That was, until the seventieth minute! Then Motherwell schoolboy Peter McBride set George Best free. Best, already a full international, used a technique favoured of great strikers like Jimmy Greaves, running the ball up close to the 'keeper and then passing the ball into the net with minimal backlift. On this occasion he nearly overdid it, for Hicks got a hand on the ball but could not divert it wide of the post. As the game drew to its close Manchester continued to dominate, but were unable to break the Swindon defence again.

There had been hopes that George Best might have been absent for the return but he flew back from international duty to help his club team. Swindon played Denis Peapell as an extra defender in the second leg at Old Trafford and at first the ploy worked. Just before half-time, however, Sadler scored the first of a hat-trick of goals and United went on to a 4-1 win with Town's sole reply coming from Bruce Walker, meaning United won the trophy 5-2 on aggregate.

SWINDON TOWN YOUTH
v. MANCHESTER UNITED YOUTH

Swindon Town Youth. From left to right, back row: Griffin, Ling, Hicks, Prosser, Foscolo, Brown. Front row: Rogers, Peapell, Plumb, Tabor, Walker.

Swindon Town: Hicks; Foscolo, Ling; Griffin, Brown, Prosser; Rogers, Peapell, Plumb, Tabor, Walker.
Manchester United: Rimmer; Duff, Noble; McBride, Farrar, Fitzpatrick; Anderson, Best, Sadler, Kinsey, Aston.
Attendance: 17,000

Swindon Town v. Northampton Town

Swindon Town 4 Northampton Town 2
Football League Second Division 23 March 1965

___

By March 1965, the heady days of the previous season when Bert's Babes had topped the Second Division seemed a distant memory and the words of my Geography teacher, Mr Lacey, that the success they were enjoying would be ephemeral, seemed all too true. Bobby Woodruff and Cliff Jackson, two of the local youngsters had departed and Swindon were struggling against relegation. They could scarcely have had tougher opponents than Northampton who only needed a point to return to the top of the table and were very much Swindon's bogey team of the period.

The fears of the home fans in the 17,686 crowd that Swindon were enjoying the luck of a relegation side seemed all too justified when, after five minutes of almost constant Swindon pressure, the Cobblers broke away and the unmarked Bobby Brown smashed home a right-wing centre from Harry Walden. With just over half an hour gone it was Brown who increased Northampton's lead, volleying home a corner by Tom Robson. It was a disheartened Town team that trudged back to the dressing room at half-time, yet, in truth, they had not played badly. Dennis Brown had seen his shot kicked off the line and an effort by Mike Summerbee had struck the bar. Bert Head pointed out that just a bit of extra quickness in tackling and Swindon could still get something from the game.

Less than five minutes of the second half had elapsed when Swindon got the stroke of fortune they needed. An Ernie Hunt shot was deflected by Theo Foley past his 'keeper. Two minutes later the Robins were level after Mike Summerbee dribbled down the wing and cut in to crash home a shot from the corner of the area. The game was now being fiercely contested with no fewer than twenty-two free-kicks being awarded against Northampton. It all nearly erupted when Norman Oakley went down to save in the Swindon area and referee Geoff Martin had to jump in to separate the players in the melee that followed. Swindon took the lead after an hour with a Don Rogers cross being neatly chested down and slotted home by Town skipper Hunt. Swindon's Brown was sent tumbling in the area but was denied a penalty. However, six minutes from the end, after a Hunt shot had been blocked, Rogers followed up to extend Town's lead and settle the nerves of the fans.

In his *Swindon Echo* column the following Friday Bert Head paid tribute to the contribution of the Town fans: 'Throughout the game even when we were losing by two goals I felt the crowd and the players were one. It was just as much a victory for the supporters as for the lads.' Sadly, it was a victory won at great cost. Ernie Hunt was left with a broken bone in the foot and Mike Summerbee's injured foot also kept him out of the next game. Ravaged by these injuries Swindon slipped down the table and their fate hung on the result of the last game of the season at Southampton.

___

Swindon Town: Oakley; Dawson, Trollope; Smart, McPherson, Atherton; Summerbee, Hunt, Brown, Atkins, Rogers.
Northampton Town: Harvey; Foley, Everett; Leck, Carr, Kieman; Walden, Martin, Brown, Hall, Robson.
Attendance: 17,686

Above: Snow, which had led to the postponement of the Northampton match from its original date, and a heavy pitch meant the County Ground car park was used for practice in the days leading up to the match.

Right: Testing out the snow-covered County Ground pitch.

SOUTHAMPTON V. SWINDON TOWN

Southampton 2 Swindon Town 1
Football League Second Division 24 April 1965

By the last day of the 1964/65 season Swindon travelled to Southampton with their two-year stay in the Second Division hanging by a thread. An Easter programme had produced a win over Rotherham, obtained at the expense of seeing Ernie Hunt sidelined for the remainder of the season, but little else. A win at The Dell would ensure Swindon's survival, a defeat would mean that Portsmouth, who were playing at Northampton in an evening kick-off, would require just one point to stay up at the expense of Town.

The game opened in sunshine and this, along with a dry, bouncy pitch, gave the game a definite end-of-season air. Luck was not on Swindon's side when Cliff Huxford, who had not scored for the Saints all season, tried a speculative shot from twenty-five yards which flew into Town's net. It was the worst possible start for the Robins but, backed by a large crowd of supporters who let out several renditions of *To be a Farmer's Boy*, Swindon carried the fight to Southampton. It was very much Swindon spirit against Southampton skill but the determination of Denis Brown paid off in the

Wilf Shergold, a local lad who was brought in to bolster Swindon's defence.

Half hidden by Saints' left-back, Denis Brown scores what was to be Swindon's last Second Division goal for four years.

thirty-second minute when he scored Town's equaliser. Hicks pulled off some fine saves in Town's goal while Rogers often threatened with some good runs down the wing. Terry Paine finally broke the deadlock with a well-placed shot after seventy-one minutes. This meant Portsmouth, who were playing in the evening, needed a point from their match at Northampton to stay up. Unfortunately for Swindon, with the results of other matches being known, Northampton knew they needed just one point to ensure their promotion to the First Division. The fact that the game resulted in a draw, which sealed Swindon's fate, perhaps explained why the last day of the season now sees all matches played at the same time. Not only did this Southampton match mean the end of Swindon's stay in the Second Division it also saw the final appearance in the Town side of Swindon's Footballer of the Year, Mike Summerbee, who was sold to Manchester City in the close season, and also veteran Ken McPherson who was released by Town and whose League career came to a close. What were the reasons for Swindon's failure to hold on to a place in Second Division? Bert Head was a brilliant manager of young players but the way he spent the limited amount of money available to him to strengthen key positions was questionable. Frank Haffey's appearances in goal worked out at over a £1,000 each in terms of his transfer fee. Frank Large failed to score in seven appearances at the start of the season and the lack of a regular centre forward perhaps indicated the foolishness of the sale of Jack Smith the previous season. Swindon had rotten luck with injuries, losing key playmaker and regular goalscorer Ernie Hunt for large chunks of the season, but perhaps most crucial of all was the broken leg sustained by Norman Oakley early in the opening game of the season at Bury. Town led 1-0 at the time of the injury but with no substitutes at this time the ten men with a makeshift 'keeper crashed 6-1. Those two points would have been enough to keep Town up.

Southampton: Godfrey; Williams; Hollywood; White, Knapp, Huxford; Paine, O'Brian; Chivers; Melia, Sydenham.

Swindon Town: Hicks; Dawson, Trollope; Morgan, McPherson, Atherton; Summerbee, Shergold, Brown, Smart, Rogers

Attendance: 17,331

West Ham United v. Swindon Town

West Ham United 3 Swindon Town 3
FA Cup Third Round 28 January 1967

Home advantage, an early goal giving the underdogs confidence, goals against the run of play and strokes of fortune are all associated with FA Cup upsets. None of these could have been fairly said to have happened in this clash at Upton Park, yet Swindon came away with a draw against a team which included three of the side that had won the World Cup only a few months before.

Swindon had lost their previous match by the only goal to Bristol Rovers and this, combined perhaps with a desire to adopt a more cautious approach, saw Danny Williams recall Keith Morgan. Morgan had not played a first-team match since the previous October but was recalled at right half with Roger Smart moving forward to the exclusion of Bruce Walker. This enabled Don Rogers to revert to his more normal left-wing position while Dennis Brown switched to outside right.

There was no early Swindon goal to unsettle West Ham's nerves; indeed, the first goal came from West Ham after twenty-four minutes of play. An angled ball behind the Swindon defence by Brabrook saw Geoff Hurst race in from the left and side-foot the ball towards the Swindon goal. Tony Hicks, who moments earlier had done well to keep out a much fiercer drive by the same player, got both hands to the ball but failed to hold it and saw it slip over the line. Swindon equalised two minutes later with a goal that involved passing and dribbling skills and finished with a fine shot. Don Rogers raced out of his own half, exchanged passes with Willie Penman, and then dribbled past two West Ham defenders before shooting home. West Ham restored their lead on the half hour when a Sealey corner kick was headed home by Geoff Hurst, whose well-timed run enabled him to power the ball into the net.

The second half saw West Ham playing the stylish football for which they were famous but good goalkeeping by Hicks and a fine last-ditch tackle by Stan Harland on Geoff Hurst stopped them increasing their lead. In fact, it was the Hammers' goal that had the narrowest of escapes when Dennis Brown fired a fierce shot that deflected off a defender's foot. As Jim Standen in the West Ham goal looked on helplessly the ball rolled agonisingly towards the goal line, only to strike a post and go for a corner. In the sixtieth minute 'Bullets' Brown, as he was nicknamed, fired another shot but this time with more success. Don Rogers had danced through the West Ham defence and had rounded Standen before passing it to the former Chelsea winger who, not willing to take any chances with hold-ups in the muddy goalmouth, blasted the ball into the net.

When Swindon took the lead twelve minutes later, it was the recalled Morgan who sparked the move. He had been doing well in defence and, as the home side seemed to tire, he became more able to prompt attacks. It was he who carefully found Brown on the right. Banking on the pace of Rogers, Brown fired a ball between the West Ham defenders. Sure enough, with the speed of a cobra strike, the man from Midsomer Norton was there, taking one touch to kill it and another to strike it powerfully past Standen into the Hammers' goal. West Ham were stunned and Town looked the more likely side to score, and it took a fine save by Standen to stop the now-rampant Brown increasing the Town's lead, but in the seventy-seventh minute Brian Dear, in the Hammers' line-up only because of an injury to Johnny Byrne, hit a left-wing cross which Hurst managed to head just out of the reach of Hicks to earn a replay they must have felt happy to get.

West Ham United v. Swindon Town

Tony Hicks in the Swindon goal pulled off some fine saves despite being beaten three times.

Although Hurst scored a hat-trick, Sam Bartram gave the accolade of Man of the Match to Don Rogers. In his *Sunday People* report he wrote 'This kid, yesterday, was worth every pound, penny and shilling any club could raise.' Swindon had other heroes as well. Mel Nurse, a Welsh international, was not overawed by the company of so many international opponents and his calm authority oozed out to the defenders around him. Two others who should be mentioned are Brown, who had taken to an unfamiliar role with surprising ease, and, last but not least, Tony Hicks, the great enigma. If you were to draw an identikit picture of the last man you would want in goal you would come up with a Hicks lookalike: short, stocky and clad in a sweater two sizes too large. A taller 'keeper would probably have saved two of the West Ham goals but a less instinctive one might have conceded three or four more.

In the replay West Ham again equalised with a late goal, Sissons' shot from the edge of the area levelling up Willie Penman's first-half goal, but Swindon surged back with two late goals by Don Rogers and Ken Skeen to show that their display the previous Saturday had not been a one-off. Most neutral observes felt that over the two matches in a clash of two good teams, Swindon had emerged as slightly the better.

West Ham United: Standen; Bovington, Burkett; Peters, Bickles, Moore; Brabrook, Sealey, Dear, Hurst, Sissons.

Swindon Town: Hicks; Thomas, Trollope; Morgan, Nurse, Harland; Brown, Penman, Skeen, Smart, Rogers.

Attendance: 37,440

Northampton Town v. Swindon Town

Northampton Town 2 Swindon Town 6
Football League Third Division 26 November 1968

To score six goals is no mean feat for any team, but to do it on the opponents' ground and against a club which had a bit of a history as a bogey team for Swindon gave it extra spice and left Swindon supporters who had made the journey to the 'other' County Ground feel their journey had been well worthwhile.

Swindon's line-up was the usual team for the period with the exception of Mickey Blick, who was deputising at centre half for Frank Burrows, who was kept out by a septic toe. It is an interesting footnote that in this match no fewer than three one-time Swindon forwards were to be involved for Northampton: both wingers Eric Weaver and Barry Lines were former Robins, as was substitute Dennis Brown.

A rainy night had kept the crowd down but those who had braved the elements were to be treated to a feast of goals. The slippery ball was causing Downsborough problems in the Swindon goal and the visitors had a lucky escape when Barry Lines got the ball in the net only to be ruled offside. Two minutes later, in the sixteenth minute, it was Lines who hit over a flag kick to Welsh Under-23 international John Roberts, who headed for goal. Downsborough got a hand to it, but was unable to keep it out of the net. Swindon stormed back and Don Heath and Roger Smart both went close before Gordon Morritt produced the save of the match to keep out a shot by Joe Butler. Swindon pressure eventually brought a reward when Stan Harland broke down the left and curled a low cross into the path of John Smith who skilfully side-footed it home. Perhaps the goal of the game came just four minutes from half-time and it was a Don Rogers trademark. Collecting a clearance from Owen Dawson in the vicinity of the halfway line, he neatly swerved around two defenders en route to the goal and then rounded 'keeper Morritt before walking the ball into the empty net.

Two goals in as many minutes seemed to have wrapped the game up for Town. Morritt was under pressure from Smart as he attempted a clearance kick from his hands and, when he checked to try and ensure his kick was not blocked, the ball slipped from his grasp and Smart pounced to fire it in. Don Heath had been cleverly switching wings with Rogers but he now popped up in the centre and challenged Joe Kiernan, one of the survivors of the Northampton team that had risen to the First Division, for a high ball. When it dropped, Swindon's other Don, as Heath was sometimes called, reacted quickly to shoot it home. In the fifty-seventh minute Frank Rankmore found Bob Hatton to reduce the arrears and, had it not been for three fine saves by Downsborough and some good defensive work by Stan Harland, the Cobblers might have got back into the game. As it was, another trademark goal made it 5-2 when Don Heath crossed after a fine dribble down the right on to the head of Peter Noble, who directed it into the goal with a header of power and accuracy. Swindon's final goal came after eighty-two minutes and was scored by Don Rogers. It was similar to the first in that it involved a lengthy dribble but this time, just for variety, when confronted by the 'keeper he beat him with a well-placed shot. Player-manager Ron Flowers' Northampton side was a shadow of the Cobblers team of the early sixties and its back four had looked decidedly shaky, but you can only beat what is put in front of you. In difficult conditions and at a time when League Cup semi-final thoughts might have distracted them, Swindon had not only won but won well and placed themselves level on points with Bournemouth, Watford and Barrow at the head of the Third Division table.

Above left: Joe Butler. But for a fine save he could have raised the goal tally to seven.

Above right: Owen Dawson deputising for the injured John Trollope. He set up Don Rogers for one of Town's goals.

Northampton Town: Morritt; Faulkes, Fairfax; Townsend, Rankmore, Flowers; Weaver (Brown), Kiernan, Hatton, Roberts, Lines.

Swindon Town: Downsborough; Dawson, Thomas; Butler, Blick, Harland; Heath, Smart, Smith, Noble, Rogers.

Attendance: 6,827

Burnley v. Swindon Town

Burnley 3 Swindon Town 3
League Cup Semi-Final Replay 18 December 1968

Having gone to Turf Moor and come away with a 2-1 lead Swindon must have felt they had every chance of reaching Wembley with the advantage of a home leg to come. Two goals in as many minutes saw this advantage squandered and it needed a header from John Smith to force the tie to a third match. This was played at the West Bromwich Albion ground, The Hawthorns. It was to produce a match that was described by Peter Lorenzo as 'one of the most courageous and noble stories of cup fighting football it has ever been my privilege to see.' With the game only seven minutes old Swindon took the lead. Roger Smart pushed a ball into the path of John Smith. Smith was a portly figure but showed surprising speed in carrying the ball forward and unleashing a shot from twenty-five yards that flew high into the Burnley net. Swindon were well on top during the first half and on two occasions Smart might have increased the lead. After Don Rogers had skipped through a tackle by Fred Smith it took a fine save by Harry Thomson to keep out the winger's fierce shot.

At half-time the Burnley manager Harry Potts rang the changes, bringing on Mike Docherty, the seventeen-year-old son of Tommy Docherty, and this seemed to kick-start a Burnley performance. The second half saw Burnley raids become more frequent and Swindon reduced to a few counter-attacking breaks. Even so, from one of these they had a glorious opportunity to tie the game up when Peter Noble shot over the bar from inside the penalty area. A foul by young Docherty on Don Heath might well have led to his dismissal in modern-day football but referee Jim Finney was a man who relied on his personality rather than his notebook to control the game and a stern rebuke prevented any recurrence of offending. It was not until the fifty-eighth minute, when a shot by the tall and powerful Burnley winger Steve Kindon forced a save from Peter Downsborough, that Town's goal was really threatened but, as the game drew to its seeming close, the Burnley pressure mounted. With a minute left it seemed Town dreams were to be realised but as Brian Clough was wont to say, 'it only takes a second to score a goal', and with just a few of them remaining, a free-kick for Burnley appeared to have been cleared. It broke to Dave Thomas who took a swing at the ball and saw it curl past the Swindon defenders and into the net. Worse was to follow for scarcely had extra time begun when Burnley took the lead. Ralph Coates, a miniature Bobby Charlton lookalike, with hair swept across his bald pate broke down the right and crossed to Frank Casper. He totally miskicked his first effort but was able to follow up and drive the ball into the Town goal. The twin towers of Wembley, which moments before had seemed to be within touching distance, must now have seemed a distant mirage for the dejected Town players. Now, however, the Town fans took a hand. Listening again to the chants of 'Swin-don, Swin-don' on a tape of the televised highlights one can understand how Swindon found a second wind and the fresh legs of substitute Willie Penman aided by the seemingly tireless ones of John Smith drove Swindon forward. Dame Fortune now turned her back on Burnley, for when Smith drove another shot towards the Burnley goal just before the end of the first half of extra time, it struck Bellamy and rebounded into the net. The goal that decided the game came with just over ten minutes remaining. Joe Butler and John Smith had combined well but the move appeared to have broken down and been half-cleared when it fell to Noble, who confidently chested it down and smashed a blistering shot which finally gave

John Smith, scorer of Town's opening goal. Later to play for and manage Walsall, he died of a heart attack at the tragically young age of forty-nine.

BURNLEY v. SWINDON TOWN

John Smith's goal that opened the scoring at The Hawthorns.

Swindon victory. It had taken seventeen and a half hours of football but at long last Swindon were going to Wembley. Described by Brian Moore as Third Division terriers, football's country cousins' celebrations on the homeward journey were suitably homespun – no champagne, just lemonade and fish and chips!

Burnley: Thomson, F. Smith, Latchham, Thompson, Wrigley, Blant, Thomas, Coates, Casper, Bellamy, Kindon.
Swindon Town: Downsborough, Dawson, Thomas, Butler, Burrows, Harland, Heath, Smart, J. Smith, Noble, Rogers.

SWINDON TOWN v. ARSENAL

Swindon Town 3 Arsenal 1 AET
League Cup Final 15 March 1969

FA Cup finals normally saw Wembley looking resplendent in May sunshine, or if the day was cloudy at least the pitch looked immaculate. For this League Cup final, however, the Horse of the Year show and the March weather had combined to make Wembley look more like a run-of-the-mill League pitch than the 'venue of legends' the ad-men were later to term it. Neither Arsenal nor Swindon appeared in their traditional red and white kit, with Arsenal changing to yellow shirts and blue shorts while Swindon opted for an all-white outfit. Swindon's line-up showed one change of personnel from the semi-final victory over Burnley. John Trollope, already a veteran in appearance terms if not in age, returned in place of Owen Dawson. He took the left-back position, having recovered from a broken arm sustained at Hartlepool that had ended his record-breaking run of 368 consecutive appearances. This allowed Rod Thomas to resume his more familiar right-back position.

In the opening quarter of an hour, George Armstrong gave Trollope a torrid time but gradually the Swindon full-back mastered him. Centres there may have been aplenty but Armstrong was not getting past. Thomas also looked nervous on a pitch that would become familiar to him in later years as a Welsh international. After nine minutes, a superb pass by Smart found Rogers and a darting run ended with a shot stopped by the feet of Wilson. If Swindon had doubted their ability to make the game a contest before, this attack certainly gave them the confidence they needed. To the surprise of many in the crowd, on thirty-five minutes, Swindon went ahead with a somewhat bizarre goal. Ian Ure, whose performance in the centre of the Gunners' defence had been beyond reproach in the opening half hour, seemed to think that Bob Wilson was still on his line. Without looking, he hit a backpass that cannoned into the legs of the 'keeper, who had advanced and was right on top of him. Noble pushed the ball into a more central position and the ever-energetic Smart, with an expression that conveyed joy and astonishment in equal measure, ran the ball into the Arsenal net. Arsenal hit back and Peter Downsborough began to become the game's central figure, effecting several saves. However, even he was helpless just before half-time when a flick header from Bobby Gould struck the foot of a post.

The second half saw Swindon come under increasing pressure. In one ten-minute period, Arsenal forced nine corners. Geoffrey Green reported that 'for fifteen minutes it was Arsenal versus Downsborough and Downsborough won.' This was in spite of the fact that he needed to receive treatment following a challenge by Gould that was described as everything from robust to downright callous. The minutes ticked away and Don Heath, who had wasted time in legal fashion and brought much needed relief to his defence with mazy dribbles to nowhere, earned himself a booking when he kicked the ball away. Seeming heartbreak struck Swindon with just moments of normal time remaining. There seemed no danger when Downsborough came out of his goal to hack the ball away. Cruelly, it struck Bobby Gould on the chest and rebounded over the 'keeper's head and he was unable to turn as Gould joyfully smashed the ball into the Swindon net. It looked as though a slip by the man who had done so much to keep Swindon's hopes alive with a string of thrilling saves was to cost them the trophy. In fact, he had merely given an opportunity for Don Rogers to make the game memorable not just for victory but for the quality of goals. It was the first

Above: Another fine save by Peter Downsborough is watched by Frank Burrows (5) and John Trollope (far left).

Below: Roger Smart follows his shot into the net as Ian Ure and the grounded Bob Wilson look on helplessly.

Wembley Squad in Wembley Colours

The Wembley squad. From left to right, standing: Danny Williams (manager), Rod Thomas, Stan Harland, Roger Smart, Owen Dawson, Peter Downsborough, Frank Burrows, John Trollope, Don Rogers, Harry Cousins (trainer). Kneeling: Don Heath, Peter Noble, John Smith, Chris Jones, Joe Butler, Willie Penman.

of his two extra-time goals that Don rated the most difficult as he had little time to get the ball down as it bobbled round the Arsenal area, following a corner, and fire it home. The second was vintage Don. The tireless Smart gained possession and pushed a pass ahead of Rogers who was running into the opponents' half in the inside-right channel. Taking the ball on, he raced into the penalty area, dribbled wide of the advancing Bob Wilson and slotted the ball into the empty net. Manager Danny Williams said, 'I told the boys at the beginning of extra time, "It's in the bag." We are the fittest team in the Football League and we have proved it.' It was perhaps the greatest day in the club's history and provoked many memorable headlines. Swindon were the new 'Wembley Wizards.' Downsborough was 'Peter the Great' and Don Rogers was 'a bundle of talent done up in a spotless white shirt'.

Swindon Town: Downsborough, Thomas, Trollope, Butler, Burrows, Harland, Heath, Smart, Smith (Penman), Noble, Rogers.

Arsenal: Wilson, Storey, McNab, McLintock, Ure, Simpson (Graham), Radford, Sammels, Court, Gould, Armstrong.

Attendance: 100,000

NAPOLI v. SWINDON TOWN

Napoli 0 Swindon Town 3
Anglo-Italian Cup Final 28 May 1970

When they flew out to Italy for the two scheduled matches against Juventus and Napoli, Swindon can have had little expectation of finishing top of the English group, as they had already lost 2-1 to Napoli at the County Ground

However, goals by Peter Noble and Don Rogers in 1-0 wins over Juventus and Napoli respectively put Town at the top of the English sides and secured them a place in the final against Napoli. When the sides lined up for the national anthems there was little hint of the drama to come. Although the supporters' club had chartered a plane to take Swindon fans to the match there hardly seemed any likelihood of crowd trouble given the vast preponderance of Italian fans. Press reports were mainly taken up by events later in the game but it seems Swindon were very much in control from the start to the premature finish. They took the lead on the half hour with a Don Rogers corner, headed home after Trevisan in the Napoli goal failed to fist clear.

The second half continued to see Town in control, with Stan Harland, who was actually on honeymoon, commanding in the Town defence. The rotund figure of John Smith set up the second

The teams line up before the Anglo-Italian Cup final.

The breaking and throwing of concrete slabs which led to the game's abandonment.

Napoli v. Swindon Town

goal around the hour mark with a fine centre that was met and headed down into the net by Arthur Horsfield. Four minutes later, a corner from the left by Rogers dropped to Noble who cleverly hooked it into the goal. Zurlini tried a shot which struck the bar and then vented his frustration by taking a wild kick at Rod Thomas. The crowd was becoming increasingly frustrated and when two boys ran onto the pitch pursued by officials it was a curtain-raiser for what was to come. With twelve minutes of the match remaining, lumps of concrete began to rain on to the pitch. Tear gas was used in an attempt to restore order but, after a hasty conversation between the Austrian referee Paul Schiller and Tournament Organiser Gigi Peronace the game was declared at an end and the Trophy presented to the Swindon skipper. Fred Ford attempted to show the trophy to the crowd, some of whose members were now busily lighting bonfires on the terraces. Estimates of the damage were put as high as £20,000, with forty people injured. Fortunately, although they had had to run for the dressing room through a hail of missiles, and their coach was pelted with bottles as it left the stadium, none of the Swindon party was injured. For Swindon, it was the second part of an Italian double as they had won the Anglo-Italian Cup Winners' Cup earlier in the season. This had been set up to compensate Swindon as the UEFA rules prevented Swindon, as a club from outside the top flight, participating in the Fairs Cup. As it was, the club produced an attractive little commemorative set of badges to celebrate the victories in the two competitions.

Napoli: Trevisan, Monticolo, Florio, Panzanato, Bianchi, Zurlini, Improta, Montefusco, Alatafini, Hamrin, Barison.

Swindon Town: Jones, Thomas, Trollope, Butler, Burrows, Harland, Smith, Smart, Horsfield, Noble, Rogers.

Attendance: 55,000

The Town squad with the Anglo-Italian Cup and Anglo-Italian Cup-Winners Cup won in the 1969/70 season.

SWINDON TOWN v. LIVERPOOL

Swindon Town 2 Liverpool 0
League Cup Third Round 6 October 1970

'I have never run out on to our own ground without being certain we could win.' These were the words of Don Rogers before Swindon took on Liverpool in 1970. It was true that their League Cup triumph two seasons earlier meant Bill Shankly could not expect a pushover, and Liverpool were in transition between the Yeats and St John era and that of Toshack and Keegan, but they were a formidable side nonetheless.

Although the first threat to goal came when a John Smith cross saw Arthur Horsfield concede a free-kick in trying to bundle over Ray Clemence, Swindon's play in the opening half hour was edgy. A shining exception, however, was Stan Harland. Playing against a club from his native city, he in no way displayed an inferiority complex and gave Alun Evans little chance to justify his £100,000 price tag. On the half hour, Steve Heighway nearly gave Liverpool the lead but his fierce shot flashed just wide. Livermore then set up Evans but Roy Jones, Swindon's stand in 'keeper, produced a fine full-length dive to save. Minutes before half-time it was Liverpool's turn to escape. Joe Butler battled to win the ball in midfield and set Rogers away. He struck a powerful shot but Ray Clemence had advanced quickly from goal and although the shot was too quick for him to hold he did manage to position himself well and block it.

The second half saw Swindon growing in confidence and a careless pass by Emlyn Hughes saw Clemence again called into action to save from Rogers. On sixty-six minutes came the goal that opened the scoring. Peter Noble kicked a long clearance out of defence that caught Liverpool over-committed to attack. Spotting the opportunity, John Trollope outpaced several Liverpool players to reach the ball and cross it to Rogers. The man from Midsomer Norton calmly carried it forward until he had created enough of an angle to fire it across goal into Clemence's net. Swindon's delight at taking the lead was somewhat tempered by the sight of John Trollope lying injured and he had to be carried off with a torn hamstring. In fact, this injury was to pave the way for Swindon's second goal. David Dangerfield, substituting for the injured Trollope, was to start the move that gave Swindon a second goal in the sixty-eighth minute. The former schoolboy international won the ball following a Liverpool corner and carefully picked out Smith with a pass. The Town midfield general then fired a long ball down the centre. Rogers raced on to it, beating the converging figures of Alec Lindsay and Larry Lloyd. Although not encumbered with having to run with the ball, the red-haired Lindsay could not catch the Wiltshire wing wonder, who sped on to round Clemence and tuck the ball into an empty net. 'Rogers for England' chants began to alternate with cheeky ones of 'easy, easy'. It was never that, but in the closing stages Dangerfield nearly made it three with a well-struck shot from twenty-five yards that clipped the crossbar. If this would have been harsh on Liverpool it would have been just for a young player who on this night seemed to suggest he would be a star of the future.

After the game, Bill Shankly was irrepressible. 'It's a ludicrous result. We were all over Swindon. They are the worst side we have played this season. Then the man Rogers pops up with two goals like this.' His old teammate, the Swindon manager Fred Ford, was more reticent. His team had just defeated a Liverpool side playing their normal defence that had just conceded five goals against ten First Division teams prior to this match. For him the team had done the talking.

Roy Jones, understudy for Peter Downsborough in this game and the match with Napoli, kept a clean sheet on both occasions.

Above: Tommy Smith (4) and Emlyn Hughes (8) provide cover for Liverpool as Frank Burrows and Arthur Horsfield look on. The girders of the new stand can be seen rising above the original stand, built in 1900 and affectionately called 'the cowshed'.

Opposite: David Dangerfield showed great promise as a teenager but never established himself as a first-team regular.

Swindon Town: Jones, Thomas, Trollope (Dangerfield), Butler, Burrows, Harland, J. Smith, Gough, Horfield Noble, Rogers.
Liverpool: Clemence, Lawlor, Lindsay, Smith, Lloyd, T. Smith, Hall, Evans, Heighway, Livermore, Withal.
Attendance: 23,992

SWINDON TOWN v. BIRMINGHAM CITY

Swindon Town 2 Birmingham City 0
FA Cup Third Round 13 January 1972

The 1972/73 season had not been a happy one for Swindon. They were struggling in the lower reaches of the Second Division as manager Les Allen sought to restore the glory days of just a couple of seasons earlier, but with little in the way of funds available. A home draw against Freddie Goodwin's Birmingham side from the First Division must have seemed a daunting prospect. Birmingham were led by former Town skipper Stan Harland, who was confident his new club would defeat his old. 'Donald would have been the only man we might have feared,' he commented before the match, a reference to Don Rogers who had by now been sold to Crystal Palace for a club-record fee of £150,000. There were two pretenders to Rogers' crown: Dave Moss and Tommy Jenkins, and both went close in the opening stages as an attacking Town line-up dominated the early stages. In a half of few chances, however, it was Trevor Francis who nearly put the Blues in front, collecting a pass from Garry Pendrey and firing a shot inches over the bar. Francis, who was to go on to win England and European honours, looked dangerous again when he attempted to dribble through the Town defence only to be halted by a well-timed tackle from John Trollope. When Swindon went close, it was thanks to an effort by Birmingham player Malcolm Page, whose rising header under pressure from Peter Noble only just cleared the City crossbar. Just before half-time, Noble himself went close. Fed by Joe Butler, he shrugged off the powerful Roger Hynd but his chip shot was just too high.

Swindon had enjoyed the better of the play in the first half, but created few chances in the second. They began to open up their visitors and young Dave Moss, who had been criticised by his manager for a lacklustre performance in the previous match that Town lost 3-0 at Bristol City, began to rip the Birmingham defence apart with some pacy runs down both flanks. In the fifty-second minute, Moss broke down the left and crossed for Joe Butler, who hit a rising shot into the Birmingham goal. City brought on Bob Hatton as an extra forward but this did not deter Swindon, who continued to press forward looking for a second goal. Butler returned the compliment of the cross for the first goal by finding Moss with a well-placed pass. Swindon, lifted by the crowd, were beginning to play with confidence and Tommy Jenkins, cleverly beating Hope, exchanged a one-two with Noble only to be stopped by a sliding tackle from Page just before he could get a shot in. The winger from Witney took the ball on into the area and as he rounded Dave Latchford was brought down by the 'keeper, who grabbed his ankles. Irish international Ray Treacy made no mistake with the spot kick to round off a fine, if unexpected, Town triumph. The fact that various papers viewed Dave Moss, Frank Burrows or Joe Butler as their Man of the Match is perhaps indicative that this was a solid team performance in which every player contributed. The fourth-round draw sent Town to the City Ground in Nottingham, where Brian Clough's Forest side eventually ran out 4-1 winners, though not before a Dave Moss goal had given them some worries.

Swindon Town: Allan, Thomas, Trollope, Butler, Burrows, Potter, Moss, Bunkell, Treacy, Noble, Jenkins.
Birmingham City: D. Latchford, Page, Pendrey (Hatton), Want, Hynd, Harland, Smith, Francis, B. Latchford, Hope, Taylor.
Attendance: 17,375

Dave Moss, creator of both Swindon goals.

Swindon Town v. Everton

Swindon Town 2 Everton 2
FA Cup Fourth Round 29 January 1977

A crushing 5-0 victory over a Fulham side containing George Best, Bobby Moore and Rodney Marsh was well rewarded when the fourth-round draw gave Town a plum home tie against Everton. Swindon lay just below halfway in the Third Division and, although Frank Burrows had begun assisting Danny Williams in a coaching role and something of a recovery from earlier disappointments was underway, First Division Everton were clear favourites despite being under caretaker manager Steve Burtenshaw. Swindon hopes were strengthened by the return to the team of Colin Prophett at the centre of the defence. This was the only change from the Swindon team in the previous round, with Tony Taylor relegated to the subs bench.

In the early stages it was Prophett's central defensive partner who came to Swindon's rescue on two occasions. A bit of ageing CND graffiti: 'What would happen if they dropped the Atom bomb on Swindon?' had been answered underneath: 'Aizlewood would head it over the bar.' One could believe it, as twice he thundered in to head away from Bob Latchford. No quarter was being asked or given and Aizlewood found his way into referee Tony Reynolds' book for obstruction. From the resulting free-kick Latchford appeared to kick Jimmy Allan as he lay on the ground and the Everton leader and Prophett became involved in a confrontation. Terry Darracott ended up in the referee's notebook when he scythed down Town winger Dave Moss. Andy King, playing at a ground where he could little have imagined he would one day be manager, created a chance for Latchford but Allan did well to punch clear. The first goal of the tie came when Darracott lobbed the ball into the path of Duncan McKenzie. The Everton man cleverly chipped the ball over Allan, and despite the latter's attempts to grasp him round the neck, toe-poked the ball home after twenty-four minutes. Town drew level just six minutes later. Ray McHale, rated Man of the Match by more than one reporter, won a free-kick for obstruction. The free-kick was tapped by Wilf Dixon to Moss, who laid it off to McHale. The stocky midfielder struck a powerful shot from the edge of the area. Lawson, in the Toffees' goal, got down to it but failed to hold it and Dave Syrett raced in to slot the ball over the goal line.

The second half almost started disastrously for Swindon, following a slip by Prophett. This allowed the artful English international McKenzie in and Jimmy Allan did brilliantly to hold on to his shot, despite having to twist in mid-air. Everton did take the lead in the fifty-first minute when a corner dropped in the Town area and was back-heeled into the path of Bob Latchford who fired home. In the sixty-first minute came the most memorable moment of the match and, for most Swindon fans, of the season. In Dave Moss and Trevor Anderson Swindon had two real wingers at a time when they were rapidly going out of fashion. It was the former who had made a clever attempt to dribble through but had been dispossessed and the ball cleared. It fell to Ken Stroud. London-born but Swindon-bred, he unleashed an unstoppable effort that Brian Madley described as 'the sort of cannon shot that deserved to win the Battle of Trafalgar'. It flew into the Town End net and was enough to earn a lucrative replay.

When this match was played just a few days later, Gordon Lee had taken over as manager at Everton. His side looked to be heading out of the cup after seventy-nine minutes, when Trevor Anderson put the Robins in front. Sadly, two minutes later Martin Dobson, who some years later was to be interviewed for the manager's job at Swindon, equalised and full-back David Jones fired his first ever goal for Everton moments before the final whistle to win the tie.

 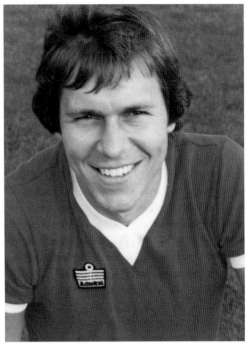

Above left: Ray McHale, whose shot opened the way for Dave Syrett to score.

Above right: Ken Stroud's equaliser picked up Central TV's award for Goal of the Season.

Swindon Town: Allan, McLoughlin, Prophett, Aizlewood, Trollope, Dixon, McHale, Stroud, Anderson, Syrett, Moss.

Everton: Lawson, Darracott (Hamilton), Lyons, McNaught, Jones, King, Dobson, Rioch, McKenzie, Latchford, Goodlass.

Attendance: 24,347

Oxford United v. Swindon Town

Oxford United 3 Swindon Town 3
Football League Third Division 26 December 1977

'With Micky French still injured and Trevor Anderson transferred, our squad looks a little thin', was the comment of manager Danny Williams before the Boxing Day derby match at the Manor Ground. In this situation, the news that Steve Aizlewood had recovered from an ankle strain came as a great boost for Town. Both sides were in a mid-table position but a game against the local rivals was enough to make it a match both sides desperately wanted to win.

The diminutive Dave Cunningham almost gave Town a dream start after five minutes when he lashed in a fierce shot which John Milkins in the Oxford goal did well to save. Play switched to the other end and the alert Peter Foley nipped in on a back pass by Colin Prophett and although forced out to a narrow angle having rounded Jimmy Allan, slid the ball into the net. Colin Prophett almost made amends soon after but Milkins reacted quickly to fist the ball over the bar. There seemed no danger when Allan jumped to collect a cross from Jason Seacole, but the Scot managed to drop the ball right onto the feet of Foley, who grabbed his second goal of the game. Six minutes later, another blow for Swindon saw Steve Aizlewood forced to leave the field with a recurrence of ankle trouble and Roy Carter was pushed into the fray. Minutes later, the game seemed over as a contest, when Allan and Prophett collided in a piece of Keystone Cops defending that allowed the gangling Ian Scott, a teenager from Wallingford, to score on his debut.

Apart from the defensive blunders, Town had not played that badly, but this made little difference to the Town fans, who heckled their manager, no doubt aggrieved at the sale of Anderson to Peterborough for £23,000 just fourteen days earlier. Five minutes into the second half, a glorious twenty-five-yard drive by Kamara found the net and sparked a revival. Kenny Stroud had reverted to the back four following the injury to Aizlewood and substitute Carter, alongside Ray McHale, began to dominate the midfield. After seventy minutes, John McLaughlin sent over a long cross, Chris Guthrie dummied to play the ball and poor marking left Kamara time and space to pull the ball down and drive it past the helpless Milkins. All the action seemed to be centring around Kamara, who had only ceased to be a teenager on his birthday the previous day. Minutes after his second goal, he was booked, but with around a quarter of an hour left to play he sent over the cross that enabled Guthrie to get in behind Colin Clarke and head the Swindon equaliser. The lively Secole nearly ruined Swindon's comeback, but the veteran John Trollope just managed to get the ball away from him as the two raced towards the Swindon goal. It may not have been the best local derby the two sides ever contested, but it was certainly good entertainment and no one went home a loser.

Oxford United: Milkins, Fogg, Stott, Clarke, Drysdale, Jeffrey, Taylor, Duncan, McGrogan, Foley, Seacole.
Swindon Town: Allan, McLaughlin, Aizlewood (Carter), Prophett, Trollope, Kamara, McHale, Stroud, Cunningham, Guthrie, Moss.
Attendance: 8,746

John McLaughlin, whose cross led to the second Town goal.

Chris Guthrie, who headed Town's equaliser.

ROTHERHAM UNITED v. SWINDON TOWN

Rotherham United 1 Swindon Town 3
Football League Third Division 24 February 1979

For Swindon the 1978/79 season had been characterised by some good displays of football but ones which lacked the killer punch. It was this lack of goals that persuaded manager Bob Smith to pay Watford £80,000 for Alan Mayes. At a time when there were still only two points for a win, the gap between them and second-placed Shrewsbury, seven points ahead, seemed large but, with two games in hand, some hopes of promotion still remained. With Rotherham a point behind Town in the table and Mayes making his first-team debut, the match at Millmoor was viewed with interest.

The game was only twelve minutes old when a nasty collision took place between Brian Williams and Richard Finney, which resulted in both players taking no further part in the contest. Home manager Jimmy McGuigan and Town boss Smith both came on to the pitch at this point not to complain about this incident but because they were concerned about a colour clash. Rotherham were wearing their normal Arsenal-style strip of red with white sleeves while Town wore a white strip with a diagonal red stripe. Although in Scotland no one seems to worry about a team in green and white hoops playing a team in green with white sleeves, in England such a clash does not usually occur. The referee declined to allow the players to leave the field but by the time the second half began Swindon had borrowed Rotherham's change strip and were wearing all blue. By this time Swindon were one up, having scored on the stroke of half-time. A move which had begun in Town's own half ended with Alan Mayes cracking a superb swerving shot from thirty yards.

It was a measure of Swindon's superiority that the Millers had not managed a shot on target until the fifty-sixth minute but, when they did, Trevor Phillips converted Alan Crawford's pass to bring the scores level. Swindon fans did not have to wait long to see the lead restored as, in the sixty-third minute, Ray McHale pierced the Rotherham defence to find Alan Mayes. Drawing Rotherham 'keeper Tom McAlister, he was fortunate to find the net for, although his shot beat the 'keeper, it was intercepted on the goal line by a defender who was just unable to deflect the ball wide of the post. Mayes completed his hat-trick just two minutes later following a long punt downfield by Jimmy Allan. John Flynn got a head to it but it skidded off to Alan Mayes who smartly rounded the 'keeper to make it 3-1 to Town. With Kenny Stroud and Steve Aizlewood in commanding form in the Town defence that was the way the score stayed, for the game to be won by what the *Advertiser* called an 'A-Mayes-ing' hat-trick.

Mayes scored eight more League goals before the end of the season but it was not enough to win promotion, Town finishing three points and three places behind second-placed Watford. Rotherham fell away to finish seventeenth.

Rotherham United: McAlister, Forrest, Flynn, Green, Breckin, Stancliffe, Smith, Finney (Dawson), Phillips, Gwyther, Crawford.
Swindon Town: Allan, Hamilton, Aizlewood, Stroud, Ford, McHale, Carter, Williams (Bates), Miller, Rowland, Mayes.
Attendance: 5,128

ROTHERHAM UNITED v. SWINDON TOWN

Above: Alan Mayes, who scored a hat-trick in this, his Town debut.

Opposite: Steve Aizlewood, a tower of strength at the heart of the Swindon defence.

Swindon Town v. Bury

Swindon Town 8 Bury 0
Football League Third Division 8 December 1979

It was a 5-0 hammering at Bury in October 1975 when Bobby Smith was in charge at Gigg Lane that must have been instrumental in persuading Swindon to appoint him as their manager. Not only had Bobby Smith become manager, but four of his former Bury team had joined him, namely Billy Tucker, Andy Rowland, Ian Miller and Brian Williams. On 8 December 1979 all were involved as Swindon obtained revenge for that October night at Gigg Lane.

Swindon were riding high in the League and looking forward to a fifth-round League Cup replay with Arsenal. It was hardly a surprise therefore when, with only ten minutes played, Ray McHale exchanged a one-two with Alan Mayes and cracked a powerful shot into the Bury net. Bury's approach was somewhat physical in the opening stages and prompted one of Clive King's unforgettable similes, describing Bury as 'like a teenage mugger who finds their victim is Muhammad Ali'. Swindon landed another blow to Bury when, with goalkeeper John Forrest and Carl Halford desperately trying to stop Rowland getting a header in, the ball got through to Chris Kamara who nodded home. Most critics agreed that Swindon's third goal was the best of the game with Kamara sending Miller scuttling down the wing and the low cross being controlled and swept in by Mayes. Mayes turned provider just before half-time, finding the head of Rowland who powered home a bullet header.

With eight goals going in at the other end it was a quiet afternoon for Jimmy Allen.

SWINDON TOWN v. BURY

Billy Tucker, who was playing against his old team in this match.

Four minutes into the second half it was two of the Bury 'old boys' who combined for Swindon's fifth, Williams' corner being stabbed home by Tucker at the second attempt. Chants of 'Bring on the Arsenal' were replaced with cries of 'We want six', and six it was when Rowland shot his second of the match past Forrest. A handling offence by Danny Wilson resulted in a penalty which Ray McHale slotted home. With twenty-two minutes remaining, a place in the record books seemed to be beckoning but Bury, despite being reduced to ten men when Alan Waldron was injured (the one substitute allowed already being on the field), managed to contain Swindon to just one more goal, a left-foot effort from Alan Mayes five minutes from time. The final score of 8-0 is at the time of writing Swindon's biggest post-war League win. Only 7,685 people watched the match and, even allowing for the fact that Arsenal brought more supporters than Bury, the attendance at the match with Arsenal only days later of 21,795 demonstrates that the appearance of thousands of 'supporters' for big-match occasions is not a new state of affairs at the County Ground.

Despite beating the mighty Arsenal in the Cup and scoring 50 goals in their home League games, more than any other team in the Third Division, Swindon's promotion challenge fell away and they finished in a disappointing tenth position. Bury finished in twenty-first position and were relegated.

Swindon Town: Allan, Lewis, Ford, Tucker, Stroud, McHale, Williams, Kamara (Carter), Miller, Rowland, Mayes.

Bury: Forrest, Ritson, Halford, Whitehead, Howard, Waldron, Madden, Wilson, Johnson, Hilton, Mullen (Lugg).

Attendance: 7,687

SWINDON TOWN v. ARSENAL

Swindon Town 4 Arsenal 3 AET
Football League Cup Fifth-Round Replay 11 December 1979

A David *v.* Goliath cup tie under floodlights with plenty of goals is perhaps the ideal recipe for a thrilling football match. So it proved in this game between the mighty Arsenal and Third Division Swindon. Swindon's road to the fifth round had not been an easy one. Aggregate victories over Portsmouth and Chester in rounds one and two had been followed by an away tie at Stoke where a late goal by Andy Rowland earned a 2-2 draw against the First Division side, who featured Viv Busby, later to become a coach at the County Ground, in their side. Swindon won the replay 2-1 and then faced a tricky trip to Wimbledon's old Plough Lane ground. Despite having Jimmy Allan playing with a dislocated finger that required him to play with two fingers strapped together, Swindon again won by the odd goal in three, a late score by substitute Chic Bates proving the winner. 'A good pay day but the end of the road' was the view of most Swindon fans when the draw for the fifth round sent Swindon to Highbury, where the home side had not conceded a goal in domestic competition since September. In fact, Swindon gave an excellent display. It looked as though a penalty, awarded to the home side in debatable circumstances, would prove decisive until substitute Billy Tucker headed home an Alan Mayes corner late in the game to set up what was to prove a County Ground classic.

Brian Williams shoots for goal during the game against Arsenal.

Andy Rowland scored Town's winner.

Swindon Town v. Arsenal

Swindon manager Bobby Smith kept his cards close to his chest but eventually decided to restore Roy Carter at centre half, although this meant changing the side that had won 8-0 in the previous match. This was probably due to the excellent way Carter had dealt with Frank Stapleton, the big Irish international, at Highbury. Despite some heavy rain the County Ground looked in good shape for what was to prove a fascinating match. The mean Arsenal defence conceded a goal of park-pitch standard when two defenders first left the ball for each other then went for it at the same time resulting in Steve Walford heading into his own net. This goal came after ten minutes, and after another ten minutes Swindon went two up. Andy Rowland dispossessed Liam Brady and passed to Alan Mayes. Now came that tinge of luck that all sides need in cup competitions. Mayes cut inside and unleashed a left-foot shot. A goalkeeper of Pat Jennings' quality would have probably saved it without difficulty but it just caught a slight deflection off Walford that left the Gunners 'keeper stranded.

Had it not been for a couple of smart saves by Jennings, Swindon might have increased their lead in the first five minutes of the second half but, just short of the hour mark, Brady headed home a Joe Devine cross. Swindon restored their lead to two goals when a shot by Kamara was blocked and rebounded to the transfer-listed midfielder, who then tried his luck with a header. This time Kamara was luckier, for it struck John Hollins on the head and looped over Jennings into the net. There were chants of 'We want eight' from the Swindon crowd, a reference to the previous Saturday's victory over Bury but Arsenal were to prove a much harder nut to crack. In Liam Brady, they had a £2 million-rated player whose left foot seemed to be the equivalent of Harry Potter's magic wand. A quickly taken free-kick was tapped to the little Irish schemer and he drove it home. He then set up the Arsenal equaliser with just six minutes remaining, when he curled a centre onto the head of Brian Talbot who scored the goal that took the tie into extra time.

After the game Bobby Smith described himself as too drained and numb to remember what he said at the end of full time but it just may be that he played a master stroke in switching Kenny Stroud to mark Brady. Brady had been bossing the game for the final twenty minutes, but now he found himself shackled. Moments before the Arsenal equaliser, the limping Mayes had been replaced by Billy Tucker, clearly a move to strengthen the defence but, in extra time, the freeing of Carter to roam the midfield also worked in Swindon's favour. Now the Robins came back into the game and, while the exchanges swung from end to end, they no longer looked like a fighter hanging on the ropes. Four minutes from time, Kamara drove in a shot and as it rebounded to create a goalmouth scramble it was Andy Rowland who reacted first to steer it into the net. Never was his nickname 'Handy Andy' better deserved.

Swindon Town: Allan, Lewis, Ford, McHale, Carter, Stroud, Miller, Kamara, Rowland, Mayes (Tucker), Williams.

Arsenal: Jennings, Devine, Walford, Talbot, O'Leary, Young, Brady, Sunderland, Stapleton, Holland, Rix.

Attendance: 21,795

Newport County v. Swindon Town

Newport County 1 Swindon Town 0
Football League Third Division 18 May 1982

On the last Saturday of the 1981/82 season a 3-0 defeat at Fratton Park seemed to have condemned Swindon to the Fourth Division. Then, as supporters sat in cars and coaches ready for the homeward journey, came the news that Walsall had only drawn their final fixture at Doncaster, meaning that if Swindon could win their final game they would stay up.

Newport's ground at the time, Somerton Park, was not the greatest piece of stadium architecture, with the railway line behind open terrace at one end and a greyhound and speedway track around the pitch distancing supporters from the action and reducing atmosphere, but it was quaintly different and Swindon could take hope from the fact that only the previous season they had managed to win there 2-0, despite having Andy Rowland deputising in goal for the injured Jimmy Allan. For this match, knowing only victory would ensure survival, John Trollope opted for a 4-3-3 formation which meant Howard Pritchard was included at the expense of Mike Graham. An enforced change was the inclusion of Gary Williams at left-back in place of Kevin Baddeley, who was suspended having amassed twenty penalty points, with Brian Hughes taking Williams' place in midfield.

Swindon's plan was to keep it tight in the first half and become more adventurous in the second. By half-time the plan seemed to be working well. Jimmy Allen had not really been troubled in the Town goal, while Mark Kendall had pulled off an outstanding save after just eleven minutes when he tipped over a curving shot from Gary Emanuel. He did even better in the second half, keeping out a fierce drive from Paul Rideout in the fifty-third minute and then diving to his left to fist out a header from Russell Lewis after sixty. Even more agonisingly for the Robins, after sixty-seven minutes, Kendall was helpless when Paul Rideout raced wide of him and screwed back a shot that rebounded off the post. Much drama remained for the last fifteen minutes however, and a lot of it centred around Roy Carter. Carter had played many great games for Town but, sadly, this was not one of them. Just two weeks before, he had missed a penalty in the home match with Newport which could have earned two precious points in a game that finally ended drawn, and now he was to be involved in incidents at both ends of the field that sealed Swindon's fate. Firstly, he had a chance with a header but, in trying to make sure of putting the ball far enough away from the formidable Kendall, he only succeeded in heading the ball wide of the post. Two minutes later, in the eightieth minute, Jimmy Allan had done well to block a shot, and the ball was crossed back into the area. Nobody was near Carter and no danger threatened as he jumped for the ball with arms stretched. The ball struck the Cornishman's arm in one of those incidents where a referee has to decide, did arm play ball or vice versa? On this occasion, the referee decided on the former and Tommy Tynan made no mistake from the spot to send Town into the Fourth Division for the first time in their history.

Whatever their failings during the season, on this night, Town were desperately unlucky. Even Newport manager Colin Addison admitted 'If we had lost 3-1 we could not have complained.' Two abiding memories of the sad night are of Charlie Henry seizing the ball out of the net following Newport's penalty, a typical example of the never-say-die spirit he would show throughout his time at Swindon, and a heartbroken John Trollope sitting alone in the coach before the journey back up the M4. Happily, both men were to share in Swindon's success in the years that lay ahead.

Above: The cover of the match programme showing the old Somerton Park ground. Surrounded by a dog track, it was not the greatest example of football architecture but is sadly missed nonetheless.

Opposite: The defeat at Somerton Park was perhaps the unhappiest night of John Trollope's managerial career.

Less happy was the behaviour of many who had followed Swindon to Newport that night. Two policemen ended up in hospital and fifty-one arrests were made as, in the ground, fencing was pushed down and, outside it, cars were attacked. One of those arrested showed a remarkable lack of common sense, appearing in court in a T-shirt proclaiming 'Official Hooligan'. Not surprisingly, he was found guilty of threatening behaviour and criminal damage.

One cannot lay this match to rest without noting that it was the last of 313 Town appearances for Kenny Stroud. Despite being voted the Town's Footballer of the Year he had been offered reduced terms and decided to go elsewhere. It was sad that a player of such elegance and consistency could not have been granted a fonder farewell.

Newport County: Kendall, Walden, Relish, Davies, Oakes, Johnson, Vaughan, Lowndes, Tynan, Aldridge (Bailey), Elsey.

Swindon Town: Allan, Henry, Williams, Emmanuel, Lewis, Stroud, Hughes, Carter, Rideout, Rowland, Pritchard.

Attendance: 5,906

SWINDON TOWN v. CHESTER CITY

Swindon Town 4 Chester City 2
Football League Fourth Division 7 April 1986

Swindon went into this game knowing that they needed just one point to clinch promotion. Visitors Chester were lying in second place and were expected to make Swindon fight all the way. Swindon had been struck a blow when Colin Gordon was ruled out with a chest complaint but Charlie Henry, who was to finish the season as Town's leading scorer, made a solid replacement. The game had an explosive opening. Only four seconds after the kick-off and with the ball not yet out of the centre circle, Steve Johnson found himself in David Axcell's book for a lunging challenge on Chris Kamara. Johnson, described by Clive King as 'a man with tree trunk thighs', had been involved in the collision several years earlier that had ended Jimmy Allen's career at Swindon, and now he made himself even more unpopular with Swindon fans when he drove home a fluffed clearance punch by Kenny Allen. The first half had only three minutes left when Swindon managed to equalise. Brian Wade, Leigh Barnard and Dave Hockaday combined well to give Dave Bamber the opportunity to head home. Incredibly, Swindon were no sooner level than they fell behind again. Peter Coyne, a player seldom found in his own penalty area and not renowned for rough tackling, was judged to have brought down Milton Graham and a penalty was awarded. Drama mounted as Johnson 'scored' only to be ordered to retake the kick due to encroachment. He held his nerve well and flashed the kick into the roof of the Town net.

The second half opened with John Butcher, in the Romans' goal, producing a fine save from Charlie Henry but, after fifty-one minutes, Town equalised again. Barnard put Hockaday away down the flank and his far-post cross enabled Bamber to head his second goal of the game. Chants

The Swindon squad during the record-breaking 1985/86 season: From left to right, back row: John Trollope (assistant manager), Leigh Barnard, Chris Kamara, Dave Bamber, Colin Gordon, David Cole, Kenny Allen, Charlie Henry, Colin Calderwood, Dave Hockaday, Andy Rowland, Chris Ramsey, Kevin Morris (physio). Front row: Brian Wade, Peter Coyne, Paul Roberts, Lou Macari (manager) Derek Hall, Tony Evans, Dave Moss.

Brian Wade dives to head Town's third goal.

of 'Going up' began to ring out from the Swindon fans and, as so often under the Macari regime, the longer the game lasted the more powerful did his side seem to become. First, a couple of body swerves took Peter Coyne into the area and his lobbed cross was met knee-high by Bryan Wade who dived to head it in. Then, with sixty-seven minutes gone, Swindon went further ahead. A left-foot cross by Henry eventually found Barnard, who got the ball under control and made space to shoot a goal that made it 4-2. A late challenge by Graham on David Cole sparked an angry reaction from Chris Kamara, who appeared to tread on the prostrate Chester player, but Graham was soon safe from further harm. He had been booked for time-wasting in the first half and now picked up his second yellow card, which ended his participation in the game. Kamara appeared to be laid out by the arm of Chester's Gary Bennett but play continued and Swindon were awarded a penalty as Wade was hauled down by Barrett. Coyne took the kick, but Butcher managed to save with his legs. It was not to be an important miss, for Swindon had the victory and the points needed to bring them back to the Third Division. By the end of the season further triumphs, in the shape of the Fourth Division Championship, clinched in a draw at Mansfield, and a record number of points in a League season, had been achieved, but it was the victory over Chester which ensured that Swindon's long decline had at last been put into reverse.

Swindon Town: Allen, Ramsey, Hockaday, Barnard, Cole, Calderwood, Coyne, Henry, Bamber, Wade, Kamara.
Chester City: Butcher, Glenn, Barrett, Greenough, Butler, Coy, Kelly, Graham, Johnson, Houghton, Bennett.
Attendance: 12,360

WIGAN ATHLETIC v. SWINDON TOWN

Wigan Athletic 2 Swindon Town 3
Third Division Play-Off Semi-Final First Leg 14 May 1987

It was the first leg of the Third Division Play-Off semi-final which saw Swindon struggle to keep alive hopes of a second consecutive promotion. The game started badly for Swindon when, with only two minutes gone, an unstoppable twenty-yard effort from Chris Thompson screamed into the Town net. Worse followed after a quarter of an hour, when the normally so-reliable Fraser Digby allowed a free-kick to squirm out of his grasp and Northern Ireland international Bobby Campbell won the race to the loose ball to increase Wigan's lead.

Perhaps the key moment of the match came early in the second half. Paul Jewell shot from close range but the razor-sharp reactions of Fraser Digby in blocking the shot and the quick response of Colin Calderwood in hacking the ball to safety kept the score at 2-0. Lou Macari's sides were noted for their fitness, and as the game wore on Swindon came more and more into the game and the benefits of the hard slogs up Liddington Hill in training began to show. Dave Bamber was foiled, due to a fine save from Roy Tunks in the Wigan goal, but three minutes later Swindon scored. Jimmy Quinn was put through on goal by a neat pass from Peter Coyne. Tunks dived at Quinn's feet and as the ball broke free Dave Bamber followed up to score. After eighty minutes came the goal that sent the Swindon fans, who made up more than a third of the crowd, dancing the conga. Steve Berry played only a handful of games for Swindon but in this one he made a vital contribution to the club's rise. After a quick word with Jimmy Quinn, he delayed his free-kick until the tall Irishman was moving into the area and then hit a sweetly timed chip onto his head. Quinn met the ball on the move and headed it firmly home. The Robins were now rampant, with Chris Kamara a dominating figure in the midfield. Two minutes from time, a Quinn pass found Mark Jones, once of Oxford but now of Swindon, and he curled in a centre from the right. Peter Coyne had once been rejected by Wigan, a decision they must have regretted when his slight figure rose to head home, giving Swindon an improbable 3-2 victory. The second leg ended goalless and set up a two-leg play-off final against Gillingham.

Wigan Athletic: Tunks, Butler, Knowles, Hamilton, Cribley, Beesley, Lowe, Thompson, Campbell, Jewell, Griffiths (Hilditch).
Swindon Town: Digby, Hockaday, King, Jones, Parkin, Calderwood, Bamber, Kamara, Quinn, Coyne, Berry.
Attendance: 6,718

Above: Dave Bamber celebrates scoring Swindon's equaliser.

Right: Chris Kamara, who made 46 appearances during the successful campaign of 1986/87, seen here in his subsequent career as a television pundit.

GILLINGHAM v. SWINDON TOWN

Gillingham 0 Swindon Town 2
Third Division Play-Off Final Replay 29 May 1987

The game began at a furious pace and Tim Parkin had twice headed clear from Gillingham corners before Steve White gave Town the lead in the second minute. A free-kick awarded for offside was played long by Phil King, and Charlie Henry, in the side due to an injury to Jimmy Quinn, rose to nod the ball on to White. Taking the ball in his stride he raced on, outpaced Les Berry and fired past his former teammate Phil Kite in the Gills' goal. The pace increased and so did the passing errors as tension and speed contributed to some scrappy play with both sides battling for supremacy in the midfield. One player who stood out in this period was Trevor Quow. Stocky but surprisingly mobile, he was the prompter of many Gillingham attacks. Just before half-time he received the ball from Karl Elsey and played a quick return that set Elsey free to turn inside Phil King, but his shot passed just outside the far post.

The second half saw Gillingham establish territorial supremacy. Fraser Digby did well when he was forced to go full-stretch to keep out a header by Irish international Tony Cascarino. Minutes later he could only watch when a shot from Dave Shearer whistled over the bar. After sixty-five minutes came a well-constructed goal that gave Town a cushion. Leigh Barnard, who had been industrious throughout, found Steve Berry, who played the ball down the left to Dave Bamber. The tall striker came out best in a tussle with his brother-in-law Greenall before chipping a pass to White. 'Chalky' took it on his chest but in adjusting to control it nearly lost his balance. He recovered quickly to run on and hit a superb shot from an angle that found the roof of the Gillingham net. With nothing to lose, the team from Kent poured forward. Digby was now under intense pressure, holding a shot from former Robin Howard Pritchard which kicked up off the turf, clutching a shot from Quow to his chest and fisting a Cascarino header away from the Town net.

Steve White, who cost just £5,000 when he signed from Bristol Rovers, scored both the goals in the victory at Selhurst Park.

Tim Parkin, whose previous experience of a European Cup final with Malmo must have stood him in good stead for the tense play-off decider.

Gillingham's growing frustration was shown as Shearer was booked for taking a kick at Bamber, and when the same player lofted over an open goal from close range, Swindon sensed victory. The final whistle was followed by scenes of joy as Town boss Lou Macari ordered his players back onto the pitch to salute the large contingent that had made the journey to South London. The first thoughts of Macari, a passionate but also a compassionate man, were for Gillingham, commenting: 'Nothing can compensate for the feeling of disappointment in the Gillingham dressing room at this moment.' He called on the authorities to scrap the play-off system, saying 'I never want to go through that again. If the authorities care anything about the game then they should call a halt to the play-offs now.' As we now know, finance has triumphed in ensuring that they are not only kept but that one game and even one penalty kick can be the arbiter of a season's fortune. Below the stands at Selhurst Park, Town chairman Brian Hillier shook hands and congratulated his fellow directors. They also received praise from Lou Macari, who acknowledged the freedom he was given in running the club in comparison to his early days in charge when 'there used to be ten board meetings a week' and he knew even a small overspend on an overnight stay would see him on the carpet. On this night well might the board have quoted the song from *Evita*: 'When the money keeps rolling in you don't keep books. You can tell you've done well by the happy grateful looks.'

Gillingham: Kite, Haylock, Pearce, Berry, Quow, Greenall, Pritchard, Shearer, Robinson (Smith), Elsey, Cascarino.
Swindon Town: Digby, Hockaday, King, Coyne, Parkin, Calderwood, Bamber, Berry, Henry, White, Barnard.
Attendance: 20,000

Sunderland v. Swindon Town

Sunderland 0 Swindon Town 1
Second Division Play-Off Final 28 May 1990

To have your captain (in this case Colin Calderwood), chairman and former manager arrested in a dawn swoop organised by the Inland Revenue on suspicion of defrauding the tax men is hardly the best build up for the play-offs, yet this was what Swindon had had to overcome to earn their place in the bright sunshine at Wembley. Swindon had finished in fourth position and earned their place in the final with two victories, by the same margin of two goals to one, over Blackburn. Sunderland's North-East neighbours Newcastle United must have been greatly disappointed not to be Town's opponents. They had finished six points ahead of the teams finishing fourth, fifth and sixth but lost out in the two-leg semi-final play-off to the Wearsiders.

The first five minutes of the match belonged to Sunderland. Had Marco Gabiaddini been just a fraction taller he might have been able to head home Eric Gates' cross, and when McPhail headed the ball down into the danger area no one was on hand to fire home. After this, Swindon began to dominate the game with the neat passing movements which were the trademark of Ardiles' sides. Steve White was proving a livewire up front but when it came to finishing he was out of luck. Four times he might have scored inside the first half-hour, with the first opportunity coming after just six minutes when he snatched at a shot with his right foot and fired wide. There was little wrong with his shooting skills on the second and third occasions, when he hit a fierce volley that Tony Norman, who was outstanding throughout, did well to cling on to, then Shearer set up a chance with a header only for a deflection to take the ball inches over the crossbar. Most agonising of all was when he raced onto a McPhail backpass. He managed to get the ball past Norman only for it to strike the post. A goal eventually came in the twenty-sixth minute and it was midfielder Alan McLoughlin who scored it. Throughout the season he had been the attacking point of the midfield diamond formation that had confused many. Early in the season McLoughlin had been a regular scorer but had now gone three months without a goal, before he produced what was to be one of the most vital efforts in the club's history. Steve Foley threaded a pass to him and the Sunderland defence gave him time to gather it and run on goal. It proved a fatal mistake for, although still outside the area, he hit a shot that took a cruel deflection off Gary Bennett and found its way into the Sunderland net. If the goal itself had an element of fortune, there was no doubting Swindon deserved a half-time lead. However, many feared that Town would be unable to maintain their territorial supremacy in the second half and would rue the missed opportunities of the first.

In fact, the story of the second half was similar to the first, with Swindon in command, but missing chances. Duncan Shearer was put through by McLoughlin only to fire wide, and the big Scot went close again four minutes from the end, when his far-post header was tipped over the bar. In between, Steve White again threatened only to see his shot kicked off the line by Reuben Agboola, while Fraser Digby came out well to take the ball from the feet of Gabbiadini, who injured his ankle in the process. The *Daily Mail*'s reporter, Peter Jackson, wrote that Swindon 'didn't just beat Sunderland to win the play-off final, they annihilated them 1-0'. This has an odd ring about it but was true nonetheless. It was a proud moment for Colin Calderwood, nicknamed 'the prisoner from cell block H' by his mates, when he collected the play-off trophy, for he had seen Swindon rise from the Fourth Division to the First in a matter of five years.

Celebrations on the pitch after the 1-0 victory over Sunderland.

The joy of play-off victory turned to anger just ten days later, when a Football League inquiry demoted Swindon by two divisions to the Third Division for making illegal payments to players. This was despite a petition of 45,000 signatures being presented by Don Rogers who travelled all the way to Villa Park to present it. A legal challenge eventually led to Swindon getting a hearing from the FA who reduced the demotion to that of one division. This meant that the play-off victory had not been completely wasted, for being a First Division club the demotion meant Swindon were able to resume their position in the Second Division when the new season started. It had taken seventy years of League competition for Swindon to reach the highest Division and just days to lose it. Fortunately, it was not to be too long before Swindon were back to try for a third great victory beneath the twin towers and get back what had so cruelly been taken away.

SUNDERLAND v. SWINDON TOWN

Manager Ossie Ardiles (front centre) and his assistant Chic Bates (in suit) join in celebrations on the team bus.

Sunderland: Norman, Kay, Agboola, Bennett, McPhail, Owers, Bracewell, Armstrong, Gates (Hauser), Gabbiadini, Pascoe (Atkinson).

Swindon Town: Digby, Kerslake, Bodin, McLoughlin, Calderwood, Gittens, Jones, Shearer, White, Maclaren, Foley.

Attendance: 72,873

BIRMINGHAM CITY v. SWINDON TOWN

Birmingham City 4 Swindon Town 6
Football League Division One 12 April 1993

A warm sunny afternoon, a bumper crowd and Swindon looking good for a play-off spot made for the prospect of a great afternoon's football. Just how memorable the day's match was to be few could have imagined as they made their way into St Andrews or, indeed, after twenty minutes play when the match remained goalless. Then Shaun Taylor, who throughout his time with Swindon was an inspirational pillar of the defence, was forced to leave the field with blood spurting from a cut over his left eye. His value was never better illustrated than in this game, for in the seven minutes he was off the field Birmingham sprang into a two-goal lead. After twenty-five minutes, a slip by Ross Maclaren let in Andy Saville, who slipped a pass behind the defence for Dean Peer to score. Then, four minutes later, Paul Moulden fed full-back John Frain who raced through to score. Typical of Taylor was his comment that the pain of the stitches being inserted in his forehead was as nothing to the agony of hearing the exaltations of the City crowd. Shaun returned to the fray to the cheers of the Town fans and his bandaged head flew like a flag of defiance, firstly in defence and then in the Birmingham penalty area where, two minutes from half-time, he climbed above a City defender and jackknifed his body to power home a header into the City net.

Six minutes into the second half, Swindon's cause seemed lost as Saville had first enabled Moulden to round the exposed Digby to score City's third and then unleashed a twenty-five-yard shot which flew like an errant homing pigeon into the back of Digby's net to make the score 4-1. It seemed just a matter of how many the home side would score, and when a neat passing move ended with Micky Hazard, back in the team for his first full game after a cartilage operation, setting up Craig Maskell to neatly slot the ball in the bottom corner, it seemed a matter of purely academic interest. Half an hour remained, however, and Town must have taken a hint from the Birmingham anthem to 'keep right on to the end of the road'. Town hearts remained strong and none stronger than Shaun Taylor's, who astonished even his own fans by breaking out of defence and storming down the left before crossing. Andy Gosney palmed it away but straight onto the head of Dave Mitchell, who headed home to make the game a contest with twenty-five minutes still remaining. Ross Maclaren made amends for his earlier error with a superb through pass to Martin Ling that the midfielder, enjoying his second spell with Swindon, impudently back-heeled to Hazard, who squared the ball to Mitchell for the Aussie striker to net his second goal of the game. Eyes everywhere but bodies static, panic seemed to have set in among the Birmingham defenders as Craig Maskell met a corner from Paul Bodin to send a looping header into the net after seventy-eight minutes. Just to complete the day, Dave Mitchell scored perhaps the best individual goal of the day when he rounded both Trevor Matthewson and the 'keeper with a final-minute goal that set the seal on one of the greatest comebacks in the club's history and helped to steer the club onwards towards a place in the play-offs.

Birmingham City: Gosney, Clarkson (Mardon), Dryden, Matthewson, Frain, Rodgerson, Peer, Parris, Smith, Moulden, Saville.

Swindon Town: Digby, Summerbee, Bodin, Hoddle, Calderwood, Taylor, Hazard, Maclaren, Mitchell, Ling, Maskell.

Attendance: 17,903

Shaun Taylor rises to meet a free kick to score the first of Swindon's six goals.

Craig Maskell (left) scores Swindon's second against Birmingham.

LEICESTER CITY v. SWINDON TOWN

Leicester City 3 Swindon Town 4
Division One Play-Off Final 31 May 1993

Throughout their long history Swindon Town have seldom done things the easy way. This was never better illustrated than in this game. Getting there had not been easy. Despite a flying start at the beginning of the first leg of the play-off semi-final, supporters were biting their fingernails until a goal ten minutes from the end of the second leg at Prenton Park ensured a place in the final. As Swindon went into the final, a huge question mark was hanging over the future of Town player-manager Glenn Hoddle, whose name had been linked with Chelsea and whose departure was seen by many as simply a matter of time. There can be little argument, however, in both the days leading up to the match and on the pitch during it that Hoddle was totally focused on achieving promotion for the club that had given him his opportunity in English club management.

With Dave Mitchell having given up the opportunity to play for Australia, Swindon went into the match at full strength, with John Moncur, who had sustained bruised ribs against Tranmere, being preferred to Micky Hazard. Leicester City carried with them the memory of having failed in their bid for promotion at this last hurdle in the previous season, when they lost out by the only goal to a Blackburn side that had pipped Swindon to the last play-off place that season.

A sun-drenched crowd had set off a host of balloons when the teams came out and the pitch was littered with the remnants of these when the match kicked off. Swindon seemed to have the better of the possession in the first half-hour, but seldom penetrated. A moment that stuck in the mind was Paul Bodin on the left flank cutting the ball back onto his right foot and floating over a centre which the Leicester defence just managed to keep away from the incoming Mitchell. Mitchell seemed to come in for some heavy treatment and it seemed a little unjust when Nicky Summerbee was booked for a rash challenge. On the bench, John Gorman scribbled notes while physio Kevin Morris puffed on his pipe. As half-time approached, the Leicester attack became more threatening. Fraser Digby could not hold a low centre from Joachim, but did enough to push it out of harm's way. Minutes later, more good work came from the Town 'keeper when he fell on a shot struck on the turn by Oldfield. Then came the first goal after forty-one minutes. However, it was not Leicester but Swindon who scored it. A sweeping move starting down the left and then swinging across to the right ended with Craig Maskell back-heeling the ball into the path of Glenn Hoddle, who had emerged from his sweeper role. Many players would have gone for power, but Hoddle elegantly hit a curling pass, not to another player, but around Poole and into the City net.

A good end to the first half was followed by a good start to the second when, with forty-seven minutes gone, Swindon scored again. John Moncur, a constant harrier in midfield, beat one defender and then stroked a pass with the outside of his foot into the path of Maskell who was just inside the area. Setting himself up, Maskell struck a left-foot shot which flew across the face of the goal and swung into the far side of the net. Minutes later a half-cleared corner was headed back into the area and bounced between several players. While others hesitated, Shaun Taylor launched himself at the ball and headed Town into a 3-0 lead. When Steve Walsh volleyed the ball over from the six-yard line, one had the feeling this must be Swindon's day, and even when after the ball rebounded from a post moments later to Joachim, who pulled a goal back for the Foxes, one was not unduly concerned. However, when a cross beyond the far post was returned with a vertically

LEICESTER CITY v. SWINDON TOWN

Expectant Swindon fans gather before what was to be Swindon's third triumph at the old Wembley Stadium.

dropping lob just too far behind Digby, which was headed in by Walsh, panic set in. Leicester were now cutting swathes through the Town defence and it came as no surprise when Steve Thompson was put through to shoot low and hard and bring the scores level. It seemed Town would be swept away as Leicester poured forward. Then, with the game going into the last ten minutes they suddenly seemed to find inspiration and create further chances themselves. The substitution of Steve White was an inspired one, as within moments of coming on he was running parallel to the City goal and seemed to be impeded first by Poole and then by Hill causing referee David Elleray to point to the spot. Bodin fired home the resultant penalty and moments later Town fans erupted in the knowledge that the following season would see Premier League football at the County Ground. The penalty had been one of those decisions that sometimes go your way and sometimes do not but, perhaps, given the fact that off-field activities denied them promotion after their earlier Wembley play-off triumph, Swindon deserved some good fortune. They certainly could not have been said to have bought success in this season. As manager Glenn Hoddle pointed out after the game 'We have sold something like £2 million worth of players in two years and this year we have spent just £100,000 in a swap deal for Craig Maskell.'

Above: Shaun Taylor thunders in to head Town's third goal.

Right: Paul Bodin, who scored the vital penalty with just ten minutes remaining.

Leicester City: Poole, Mills, Whitlow, Smith, Walsh, Hill, Oldfield, Thompson, Joachim, Agnew, Philpott.

Swindon Town: Digby, Summerbee, Bodin, Hoddle, Calderwood, Taylor, Moncur (Hazard), Maclaren, Mitchell, Ling, Maskell (White).

Attendance: 73,802

Liverpool v. Swindon Town

Liverpool 2 Swindon Town 2
FA Premier League 11 December 1993

Anfield is not set in the most prosperous district of Liverpool but on match days it has a life of its own, with many a scouser turning their backyard into an impromptu car park. Early in the season, Town had gone down 5-0 on their own ground and John Gorman must have been dispirited by the fact that he was being asked 'How many do you think you will lose by today?' Given that Town had gone down just days before to a much less star-studded Oldham side, albeit to the odd goal in three scored in the last ten minutes, the possibility of getting any points seemed slim. The suspension of Luc Nijholt made room for Martin Ling to come back into the Swindon midfield. Liverpool, under Souness, were a bit different to the Liverpool of old: less solid in defence, but more likely to score goals. Keith Scott and Andy Mutch, a man rejected by Everton earlier in his career, both caused problems for the Liverpool offside trap. It was an end-to-end game and the first half saw Liverpool create a number of chances. That they failed to score was due to the excellence of Fraser Digby. Many factors contributed to Swindon's failure to hold on to Premier League status and the injuries that kept Digby out of the side was not least among them. The first of his saves in this game came after just two minutes, when he turned away a shot from Ruddock, but perhaps the pick of his saves was the one that kept out an effort by Steve McManaman a few minutes from half-time. Swindon responded and, had Keith Scott's header from a Paul Bodin free-kick been a yard either side, Town would have been in front. As it was, the ball thumped into the chest and grateful grasp of Grobbelaar.

Liverpool pressure was beginning to mount as they attacked the Kop end. Rush fired into the side netting and Digby had to save from Ruddock and McManaman in quick succession. An hour had been played before a goal came, and to the delight and surprise of Swindon fans it came from their team. It resulted from a large scale one-two, the one coming when Moncur hit a long ball into the path of Nicky Summerbee, the two when the latter crossed beautifully for Moncur to volley the ball past Grobbelaar. It took just eight minutes for Liverpool to draw level, a cross from Neil Ruddock being headed in by John Barnes after seventy-four minutes. Just six weeks before, Keith Scott had been plying his trade at Wycombe. Impressed by his power in the air during a pre season friendly, John Gorman had paid £300,000 for him. At Anfield, he scored his third goal in six games, making the investment seem an excellent one. When Kevin Horlock got to the byline and pulled the ball back to the far post, Andy Mutch got in a header that Grobbelaar could only block. The ball dropped to Scott who slammed the ball in, right in front of the Town fans gathered at that end of the ground. Dreams of a first Premier League away win at Anfield faded when, with just four minutes remaining, Mark Wright got in front of Adrian Whitbread for an equaliser that Liverpool scarcely deserved. Kelvin Morton was a referee who had not endeared himself to Town fans some years earlier when sending two Swindon players off at Leicester. He had controlled this match in a particularly unfussy way, however, and it seemed a shame that having kept his notebook empty until the eighty-ninth minute, he now booked Ling.

At three o'clock that afternoon, many Town fans would have gladly accepted a point from a game which seemed a home banker if ever there was one, but so close had victory come that the result was tinged with sadness. 'I'm delighted yet very disappointed,' said Town boss John Gorman. 'I felt

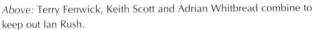

Above: Terry Fenwick, Keith Scott and Adrian Whitbread combine to keep out Ian Rush.

Right: Fraser Digby fists clear under pressure from Ian Rush, while Robbie Fowler looks on.

that with our initiative and our endeavour, we deserved all three points.' Peter Wilson in *The Times* wrote 'Liverpool fans knew the better side did not play in red', while the genuine comments of Liverpool fans that 'go on playing like that and we will see you next year' gave hope that Swindon, already four points behind Chelsea in the last of the relegation spots, might yet avoid the drop.

Liverpool: Grobbelaar, Jones, Wright, Ruddock, Harkness (Nicol), Barnes, Molby, Redknapp, McManaman, Rush, Fowler.
Swindon Town: Digby, Fenwick, Whitbread, Taylor, Bodin, Horlock, Ling, Moncur (Fjortoft), Summerbee (Maskell), Scott, Mutch.
Attendance: 32,739

SWINDON TOWN v. MANCHESTER UNITED

Swindon Town 2 Manchester United 2
FA Premier League 19 March 1994

Which team scored most goals against Manchester United in the FA Premiership season 1993/94? Amazingly, the answer to this piece of footballing trivia is Swindon Town. At Old Trafford, Swindon had conceded four goals, but Steve White, who had come on as a sub for Jan Aage Fjortoft, ensured Town did not allow United to escape with a clean sheet as his energetic style helped Swindon in the last quarter of an hour. Firstly, Bodin had crossed for Mutch to score, then he had converted a penalty after the speedy White was brought down by Steve Bruce. When the return fixture took place at the County Ground Swindon were 10:1-on for relegation and Manchester United were hot favourites to earn a victory to boost their challenge for the double of League and FA Cup. There was some bright news for Swindon in that their speedy wing-back Nick Summerbee had returned to the team after injury, while Brian Kilcline and Lawrie Sanchez were included to add experience to the Town side that had crashed 7-1 at Newcastle the previous Saturday.

Things seemed to be going according to the form book when United took the lead in the thirteenth minute. The move began with Paul Ince winning the ball in midfield and ended with Mark Hughes crossing for Roy Keane to plant a header wide of Digby's reach. It was an incident involving Hughes that brought the game to life. The Welsh striker was bent over retrieving the ball when he fell on the pitch-side track, possibly having been struck by someone in the crowd. This incident, and Hughes' angry response, raised the temperature of the match. Swindon refused to be swept aside, however, and Brian Hill's whistle was kept busy. Lawrie Sanchez earned a booking on his Swindon debut in the twenty-fourth minute and, not long afterwards, Denis Irwin was not the first full-back in the season to find himself booked after an attempt to get the ball from Summerbee. Ten minutes from half-time, Swindon drew level. There were a crowd of players between Luc Nijholt and the United goal so there seemed little danger but the Dutch midfielder's speculative effort from thirty yards took a slight deflection which left the giant figure of Schmeichel helpless as it sped into the net.

Early in the second half Hughes had a good chance to score for United but failed with a header, and Swindon responded through a good run by John Moncur that took him past three defenders before he shot wide. United regained the lead after the ball broke loose following an aerial clash between Brian McClair and Adrian Whitbread, and Paul Ince scored with a powerful shot. The incident that was to dominate the football pages the following day happened in the sixty-fifth minute. The midfield conflict between John Moncur and Eric Cantona had been rather like watching a stately Victorian lady being harassed by a small terrier. Suddenly, after Moncur had snapped at the Frenchman's heels just once too often, Cantona trod on the prostrate Swindon player. Having consulted his linesman, referee Hill, who a year earlier had been the subject of Alec Ferguson's wrath and wish that he did not referee any more United matches, sent Cantona off. It is always difficult to tell what is 'putting your foot down' when an opponent is underneath it and what is deliberate stamping, as it is basically all about intent. A similar incident had been the subject of television coverage the previous week, when close ups had shown the Frenchman standing on a Norwich player in a similar way. Had the officials seen this? Did it figure in their

Above left: Luc Nijholt fired home the first Town equaliser.

Above right: John Moncur (on ground) and Eric Cantona, in the incident that led to the latter's dismissal.

estimation of the challenge as deliberate? One can only surmise. What was indubitable was that it gave Swindon a whiff of hope that they could get something out of the game. Taylor crossed hopefully into the United box, and when the 'keeper only half-cleared the punch, a scramble developed and eventually Fjortoft poked the ball over the goal line. A point was probably no more and no less that Swindon deserved, but it did enable them to lay claim to that feat of most goals against United.

Swindon Town: Digby, Summerbee, Whitbread, Kilcline, Taylor, Horlock (Ling), Sanchez, Moncur, Nijholt, McAvennie (Scott), Fjortoft.

Manchester United: Schmeichel, Parker, Bruce, Pallister, Irwin, Cantona, Keane, Ince, McClair, Giggs, Hughes.

Attendance: 18,102

Swindon Town v. Millwall

Swindon Town 3 Millwall 1
Football League Cup fifth round 11 January 1995

Having held Premier League status the previous season, Swindon were exempted until the second round of the Coca-Cola Cup, as the League Cup was termed in this season. Defeat by three goals to one on their own ground by Charlton might have seemed to have ended Swindon's interest in the competition, but a Fjortoft hat-trick at The Valley pushed the tie into extra time during which Swindon emerged victorious. A replay victory over Brighton and a home win over Derby took Swindon into the last eight and a home tie against Millwall.

Millwall started as the bookies' favourites to win which, in view of the fact that Town had gone fourteen League matches without a win, was not surprising. The game certainly seemed to be going according to the form book in the early stages, with both Alex Rae and Mark Kennedy squandering chances before Nicky Hammond pulled out a fine save to prevent Ian Dawes from scoring. Swindon took the lead in the twenty-sixth minute with a beautiful four-man move which began with Paul Bodin finding Jan Aage Fjortoft and ended with Joey Beauchamp crossing for Andy Mutch to side-foot the ball home. Eleven minutes later, Fjortoft scored with a shot that curled around Kasey Keller from at least twenty-five yards. Millwall manager Mick McCarthy said 'If he meant that, I will go and show my backside in Burton's window', but Fjortoft was in a rich vein of form and scoring with efforts which other players would not have attempted. One began to feel it could be Swindon's night – between the two goals, former Town striker Dave Mitchell had unleashed a shot which might well have found the net had it not struck Kevin Horlock and been deflected up and over the bar.

In the sixty-first minute Swindon made the game safe when Andy Mutch scored his second of the night. Ian Culverhouse, who had played with magnificent authority in defence, started the move with a pass to Mutch, and he moved it on to Fjortoft. The tall Norwegian opened up the defence with a clever back-heel to Beauchamp who crossed for Mutch, who prodded the ball home from close range. Tempers flared off the pitch in the sixty-sixth minute when a late challenge by Kennedy on Mutch caused a confrontation between the managers that was ended by a policeman positioning himself between them. Four minutes from the end, Jason Van Blerk crossed from the left and Dave Mitchell scored with a downward header. The performance certainly impressed Phil Duffell in the *Advertiser* as he gave three players (Culverhouse, Mutch and Fjortoft) ten marks each, while all the other Swindon players got nine.

Swindon seemed to have a great chance to reach a second Wembley League Cup final when the draw for the semi-final paired them with the other surviving First Division club, Bolton Wanderers. Alas, it was not to be. The sending off of Mark Robinson for a retaliatory foul in the first leg and a late rally by the Wanderers in the postponed second leg ended Swindon's hopes.

Swindon Town: Hammond, Robinson, Bodin, Culverhouse, Nijholt, Taylor, Horlock, Beauchamp, Fjortoft, Mutch, Ling.
Millwall: Keller, Dawes, Van Blerk, Roberts, Weber, Stevens, Savage, Rae, Cadette, Mitchell, Kennedy.
Attendance: 11,772

Above: Jan Aage Fjortoft managed to curl this effort between the Millwall defenders and into the net.

Below: Andy Mutch fires home one of his two goals.

Blackpool v. Swindon Town

Blackpool 1 Swindon Town 1
Football League Division Two 20 April 1996

When Swindon ran out at Bloomfield Road for this match they had the opportunity to throw into reverse one of the most disappointing slides in the club's history. The previous two seasons had seen consecutive relegations. Now, five points clear of opponents Blackpool with two games in hand, a win would have clinched the Championship while a draw would have been enough to ensure that local rivals Oxford United could not match their points total and thus ensure Swindon an automatic promotion place. Many Swindon fans had decided to make a weekend of it, taking advantage of the fact that the match was in a holiday resort. Indeed, many local hoteliers had bought tickets for the game and then offered them as part of an accommodation package for the weekend. The Town side lined up with no change from that which had played out a goalless draw in the previous match at home to Burnley.

While Blackpool were involved in a tense struggle with Oxford, the fact that Swindon's promotion would in all probability only be a matter of time, given their commanding position, was quickly reflected in the first-half play. Swindon, playing in their away strip of dark and light-blue halves, passed the ball in an assured fashion, while Blackpool looked hesitant and at times bad-tempered. After quarter of an hour's play, Town took the lead. Mark Robinson picked out Wayne Allison with a cross and 'the Chief' calmly held the ball up before laying it back into the path of Kevin Horlock. Horlock struck it beautifully with his right foot and it rocketed into the net. But for an incident a few minutes later, Swindon might have gone on to a comfortable victory. Eric Nixon and Scott Leitch collided as they chased for a ball and the Swindon player was taken off with damaged knee ligaments. Leitch, who had impressed enough during a loan spell from Hearts to earn a permanent transfer, was a key man in the Town midfield and his loss led to a reshuffle. Wayne O'Sullivan came on with David Preece taking over the anchorman role in the Town's midfield. Around the half-hour, Blackpool enjoyed perhaps their best spell of the game with Andy Watson's shot going narrowly wide and James Quinn just failing to make contact with the ball close in on the Town goal. However, Swindon hit back and Horlock nearly added to his first goal with a free-kick which just went wide. Blackpool were becoming increasingly frustrated and Andy Preece earned himself a booking for jumping at Culverhouse, rather than the ball, in an incident which left the Robins defender requiring medical attention.

Blackpool had a glorious chance with the second half just minutes old. Quinn was left with the whole goal to shoot at but placed his shot straight at Fraser Digby. Moments later a somewhat fortuitous strike by Andy Barlow from fully thirty yards brought the Seasiders level and set the game up for an exciting finish. Swindon were pushed somewhat on to the back foot but Shaun Taylor was a commanding presence as the high balls rained in and Peter Thorne nearly snatched it for Town in the dying minutes.

After the game there was an unpleasant incident outside the changing rooms when Blackpool manager Sam Allardyce pushed away reporters waiting to see Swindon manager Steve McMahon. Perhaps his frustration was understandable given that news had come in that Oxford had defeated Bristol City. Swindon's next match saw them clinch the Second Division Championship with a 3-1 win at Chesterfield that equalled the club record of twelve away wins in a League season. Blackpool had the frustration of slipping out of second place and being pipped to promotion by Oxford.

Kevin Horlock, scorer of Town's goal.

Blackpool: Nixon, Bryan, Barlow, Linigan, Mellon, Quinn, Lydate, Bonnor, Philpott (Ellis), Watson (Brown), A. Preece.

Swindon Town: Digby, Robinson, Culverhouse, Bodin, D. Preece, Allen (Seagraves), Taylor, Leitch (O'Sullivan), Thorne (Cowe), Allison, Horlock.

Attendance: 9,175

Swindon Town v. Queens Park Rangers

Swindon Town 3 Queens Park Rangers 1
Football League Division One 5 November 1997

Swindon faced a tough task when Queens Park Rangers, who had spent several million pounds to try to reclaim a Premiership place, arrived at the County Ground. Swindon had eight first-team players on the injured list and, most notably, a goalkeeping crisis. Both Frank Talia and Fraser Digby had been on the injured list when Swindon had won their previous encounter at Portsmouth but stand-in 'keeper Steve Mildenhall had kept a clean sheet, despite having to have six stitches in his testicles after sustaining an injury pulling off one brave save. McMahon was torn between throwing in youngster Antony Betterton or using Alan McDonald as a stand-in. Steve McMahon had gone back to one of his old clubs (Liverpool) to sign Tony Warner on loan, but his registration failed to beat the deadline. McMahon's dilemma was resolved by Digby, who volunteered to play despite struggling with an injured chest.

It seemed the former Sheffield Boys 'keeper might be in for a busy night when Rangers pressed in the early stages. Two-and-a-half-million-pound striker Mike Sheron headed just over from a corner and, following another flag kick, Karl Reddy met the cross at the far post to head just wide. There was nothing Digby could do when Rangers went ahead after fourteen minutes. Trevor Sinclair crossed and Gavin Peacock sent a beautifully placed long-range header into the far corner.

This sparked a brief response from a Swindon team who had seemed somewhat diffident, when Ty Gooden fired over from fifteen yards out. Back came Rangers though, and Peacock might have scored his second but for Digby going full-length to pull off a save that would have done credit to a fully fit 'keeper, never mind one struggling with injury.

The first half had been a combative affair and after Craig Taylor had been booked for handball in the eleventh minute, Morrow, Bullock and Sinclair all followed him into the referee's book before half-time. Steve Morrow, who was giving Wayne Allison a tough time, was perhaps lucky not to receive greater punishment. The second half literally began with fireworks as they sparkled overhead from a nearby display and one spent rocket nearly fell on the head of Rangers' Matthew Brazier. Swindon's players were finding chances hard to come by, and when one did fall to Chris Hay he blazed high and wide. It was a flash of characteristic genius from Mark Walters that brought Swindon level after sixty-seven minutes. Craig Taylor found the former England international on the edge of the box and Walters' volley eluded both the grasp of Harper and the last-ditch attempt to clear off the line by Reddy. Just before the Swindon goal, a scuffle between Danny Maddix and Chris Hay had led to both players being booked. Worse followed for the Londoners, when Maddix made a late challenge on Hay and was sent off for two bookable offences. In the eighty-fourth minute, Craig Taylor scored a goal reminiscent of his brother Shaun. He admitted closing his eyes when meeting Gooden's cross but the roar of the crowd must have been enough to tell him his effort had been successful. Two minutes from time, Hay put the seal on Swindon's victory, rounding the 'keeper before slotting home a low shot. After the game, Digby, who had been worried that his injury might hamper him with shots going to his left, said, 'I can't thank the crowd enough... I do not think I could go anywhere else and feel the same warmth and kindness.' McMahon, who had urged his team to be patient at half-time, said, 'Anyone watching could see a genuine team spirit out there.'

SWINDON TOWN v. QUEENS PARK RANGERS

Above left: Harper is well beaten by Mark Walters shot for the goal that brought Town level.

Above right: Ty Gooden, seen here getting the better of a Rangers defender, was a pacy midfield player with an explosive shot.

Although two victories lay in the near future, so did the sale of Wayne Allison to Huddersfield and this night's victory may be seen as the high-water mark of the McMahon era. George Ndah, bought as a replacement, scored on a hugely impressive debut against Middlesbrough, but Town went down 2-1 and the bubble burst. Chris Hay never seemed quite the same player that he had alongside Allison, and Swindon gradually slipped down the table. Within a year, McMahon, like Allison, belonged to Swindon's history.

Swindon Town: Digby, Borrows, Culverhouse (S. Davis), Bullock, Taylor, McDonald, Watson, Walters (Pattimore), Hay, Allison, Gooden.

Queens Park Rangers: Harper, Maddix, Reddy, Morrow, Rose, Barker (Quashie), Peacock, Brazier, Sinclair, Gallen (Slade, S. Yates), Sheron.

Attendance: 10,132

SWINDON TOWN v. PETERBOROUGH UNITED

Swindon Town 2 Peterborough United 1
Football League Division Two 28 April 2001

With two Saturdays remaining in the 2000/01 season Swindon were still involved in a relegation dogfight. The fates of Luton, Swansea and Oxford had all been sealed but those of Swindon, Cambridge and Bristol Rovers still hung in the balance. Swindon and Cambridge were a point ahead of Bristol, but the Rovers had two games in hand on Swindon and one on Cambridge. With a tough away game at Stoke as the last match of the season it seemed Swindon must win if they were to stay up.

Town could hardly have got off to a better start. Only seven minutes had been played when Keith O'Halloran sent over a deep cross to the far post where Gary Alexander rose to loop a header over Mark Tyler in United's goal. Gary Alexander was signed from West Ham by Colin Todd, and the club's failure to complete the payment of the transfer fee left Andy King hamstrung by a League embargo on new signings. At the last, however, it looked as though his goal might be the one that kept Swindon up. The ever-busy David Duke broke down the left and found Matthew Hewlett, whose shot had 'goal' written all over it until Richard Scott cleared off the line. After this, Town were forced back on the defensive. Leon McKenzie would surely have scored had not Duke got in a tackle and Town old boy Martin Williams fired just past a post. After twenty-eight minutes, Alan Reeves produced a similar saving tackle to Duke's but it was sheer good fortune that the Town did not concede a goal just before the interval. Steve Mildenhall had picked up the Swindon Player of the Season award just before the kick-off but he might well have been picking the ball out of the net when Francis Green's shot struck a post and the tall Swindon 'keeper only just managed to tip the ball away as McKenzie followed up.

Six minutes into the second half came an incident which one felt should ensure a Town victory. Dean Hooper, another player who had had a short spell at Swindon, appeared to throw a punch at Steve Robinson. Referee Fraser Stretton spent a long time consulting his linesman before flourishing a red card, which sent Hooper into an absolute rage and it was perhaps fortunate that his teammates grabbed him and hustled him away before he got into further trouble. Surely Swindon would be safe now. However, when a header by Alexander from an Invincible cross rebounded off the post one began to wonder and, when a flying save kept out a shot by Robinson, doubts began to surface. As so often happens when playing against ten men, Swindon seemed unsure as to whether to push the extra man into attack or use the numerical advantage to make sure of what they had. Then came a comical schoolboy mix-up which looked likely to have dire consequences for Town. Both Reeves, who eventually poked the ball into his own net, and fellow defender Mattie Heywood were convinced that the 'keeper called, something Mildenhall denied. Perhaps the call had come from a third party! All seemed lost, with relegation seeming to have been brought about by sheer incompetence with a farcical goal conceded against ten men. Andy King threw on Ian Woan, a cool and cultured player with an explosive finish. It seemed a good move as three times he might have scored, but three times he failed. With visions of journeys to York, Darlington and Hartlepool already coming into the home fans' minds, a ball was punted down the left. Danny Invincible's pace made him first to it, as he raced into the left-hand side of the penalty area. Nine times out of ten the Aussie would have put it onto Stratton Bank but this time he 'bent it like Beckham' into the

Danny Invincible, who scored the goal that saved Swindon from relegation.

Posh goal. Whether he meant to swerve it or whether it slid off the side of his boot no one cared. Swindon had a lifeline and when the news came through that Cambridge and Bristol Rovers had lost it looked unlikely to snap. The man with the comic-strip name had produced a storybook finish which will always endear him to Town fans, even though his County Ground days are over.

Swindon Town: Mildenhall, Invincible, Willis, Reeves, Heywood, Duke, O'Halloran, Hewlett, S. Robinson (Woan), Alexander, Reedy (Van der Linden).

Peterborough United: Tyler, Hooper, Morrow, Rea (Lea), M. Scott, M. Williams (T. Williams), Farell, Hanion, Danielsson, Green (Oldfield), McKenzie.

Attendance: 8,145

READING v. SWINDON TOWN

Reading 1 Swindon Town 3
Football League Division Two 13 October 2001

There were already indications that Roy Evans' period in charge at Swindon might be a short one. The former Liverpool boss had indicated that if Mr Donovan was to lose control of the club he would have to consider his position. Such things lay in the future and the minds of most Swindon fans were focused on whether Swindon could record a first-ever victory at Reading's Madejski Stadium. Reading's new ground was certainly excellent for viewing football but the car-park charge of £4 and the fact that, in common with many new stadiums, all traffic has to leave down one road, made many long for the old Elm Park Ground.

The ground was bathed in warm sunshine and many of the crowd were in shirtsleeves as the game started, with Swindon defending the goal behind which their supporters were gathered. Adrian Whitbread and Adi Viveash were former Town players lining up for the Royals while Andy Gurney, in the Town line-up, had moved in the opposite direction. Swindon's midfield was looking calm and composed, gaining possession and passing the ball swiftly and accurately. A moment of anxiety came for Town after twenty minutes, when Nicky Forster dashed into the Town area and looked poised to score, but a fine sliding tackle by Paul Edwards dispossessed him. The twenty-one-year-old, who had been signed from Leigh RMI of the Conference, was operating in a left wing-back position and as often during his short and injury-scattered time at Town, he was a thorn in the opposition side. Also, back in the Town side was Neil Ruddock, who proved a massive influence in more ways than one. International players, even those past their prime, seem to have a knack of hitting an accurate pass be it long or short. It was the former that Ruddock was using to try to get his forwards away and, in the thirty-seventh minute, he succeeded with a pass that Giuliano Grazioli latched on to, before crashing a right-foot shot wide of former Oxford 'keeper Phil Whitehead.

Early in the second half Reading might have levelled the scores but, when Viveash headed the ball back across the Town goal, Anthony Rougier headed over from six yards out. With the second half just seven minutes old, Town increased their lead. Man of the Match Paul Edwards raced down the left, beating two defenders before hitting a centre to the far post. Danny Invincible timed his run well and just managed to nip in to head the ball down into the Reading net before two blue-shirted defenders clattered into him. Tempers began to fray a little as the game moved into the closing half-hour and no fewer than five Town players picked up bookings. With ten minutes left, Bobby Howe was dispossessed on the edge of the Reading area and a long kick forward found Darius Henderson racing through. Griemink, who had been well covered by his defenders and had little to do, raced from his goal but then seemed to hesitate, allowing Henderson a margin for error as he chipped the ball over the 'keeper, who found himself caught in no man's land. If Reading fans thought Roy Evans' ploy of sending on three subs in the last ten minutes was purely to waste time, they were proved wrong three minutes from time. The last of the subs to come on, Joe Osei-Kuffour, an on-loan striker from Arsenal, struck the goal that sealed Town's victory. Showing quick thinking, Bart Griemink in the Swindon goal spotted Reading over-committed and caught them out with a long quick clearance which Kuffour raced onto and rounded the Reading 'keeper.

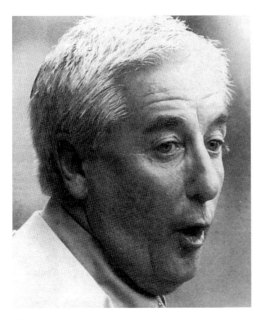

Above: Roy Evans, the Town manager who masterminded Town's victory.

Right: 'Razor' Ruddock celebrates victory following the final whistle at the Madejski Stadium.

After the game, rumours circulated that Alan Pardew had resigned. In fact he remained in charge to take Reading to promotion from Division Two and a play-off place in the higher division, while Roy Evans did not see out the year at Swindon.

Reading: Whitehead, Viveash, Williams, Shorey, Igoe (Henderson), Harper, Parkinson, Butler (Rougier), Forster, Hughes, Cureton.

Swindon Town: Griemink, Duke, Reeves, Gurney, Ruddock, Edwards (Heywood), Robinson (McAreavey), Howe, Hewlett, Invincible, Grazioli (Kuffour).

Swindon Town v. Barnsley

Swindon Town 3 Barnsley 1
Football League Division Two 10 August 2002

The weather at the County Ground on the opening day of the 2002/03 season seemed more suited to cricket than football and the shirtsleeved crowd were looking forward to the new season with guarded optimism. The position of Neil Ruddock, who had returned from the summer break slimmer but injured, was causing some dissension within the club and his wages were imposing a considerable strain on the club's limited financial resources. On the bright side, Swindon had a new striker, Sam Parkin, on display. Sam had had a good goalscoring record while at Oldham and Millwall but his loan periods from Chelsea to Northampton and Wycombe had been less successful. Fans looking for omens would have taken heart from the fact that the first time Swindon ever won a League promotion, way back in the 1962/63 season, the campaign had begun with a match against Barnsley. It was felt likely that Barnsley would prove a good test of Town's prospects, as they had only been relegated the previous season.

The early goal attempts came from Barnsley, with Mike Sheron having a goal disallowed and Kevin Betsy having a shot that rebounded off the post. Swindon's attack looked lively with the pace of Eric Sabin and Danny Invincible causing problems for the Barnsley defence but without either player ever testing the 'keeper. With both sides committed to a 4-3-3 formation it was a contest in which both sides' main intention seemed to be to score goals rather than stop them, and this was contributing to an entertaining match. At the half-hour mark, Barnsley took the lead. Stefani Miglioranzi brought down Kevin Betsy and the referee pointed to the spot. Chris Lumsdon made no mistake, but the lead was short-lived. Almost straight from the kick-off Matthew Hewlett, made captain in the absence of the suspended Andy Gurney, found Danny Invincible. The Australian picked out new boy Sam Parkin. Parkin turned on the ball, making space for a shot that he struck firmly and accurately, low into the Barnsley net. Barnsley might have restored their lead but when Gary Jones fired in a shot, Bart Griemink in the Town goal was more than equal to it.

Town took the lead in the fifty-second minute when Invincible used his pace to defeat the Barnsley defence before cutting inside to fire a shot at Marriott, which the 'keeper could only block but not hold. He might well have considered he had knocked the ball into a safe area but, showing the anticipation and coolness that is the hallmark of great strikers, Parkin seized on the loose ball and fired it in through the narrow angle that had been exposed to him. Swindon began to play some smart passing football that delighted the crowd. Steve Robinson was working busily and Miglioranzi was delighting the crowd with some perceptive long passes. It looked as though Parkin was going to be denied his hat-trick when, having got on the end of a cross from Gareth Edds and headed home, the goal was disallowed due to Matthew Heywood being offside in a central position. With six minutes remaining, Andy King brought on Jimmy Davis, who was on loan from Manchester United. He made an immediate impact, his pace and power being too much for Mike Flynn, who brought him down in the area. There could only been one possible person to take the penalty: Parkin. He made no mistake, thus becoming one of those rare individuals who have scored a hat-trick on their Town debut.

It was a happy opening to the season for the Swindon fans and there were many smiling faces as the ground emptied with a feeling that here was a side that might challenge for promotion. After a

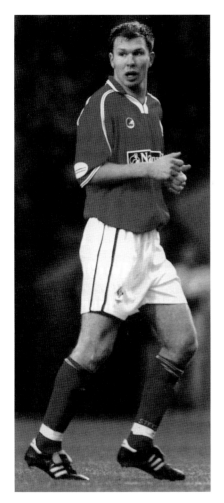 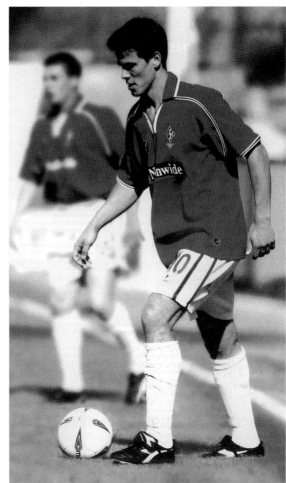

Above left: Sam Parkin, who proved a hat-trick hero on his debut.

Above right: Stefano Miglioranzi impressed with some shrewd long passes.

bright start, however, an incredible game against Stockport, which Town lost after dominating, sparked a run of poor form. This was not helped by an injury to Davis and a suspension and injury to Parkin. For a while, Andy King's job seemed in doubt but the team rallied, with Parkin ending with 26 goals for the season and the club in a comfortable mid-table position.

Swindon Town: Griemink, Edds, Willis, Heywood, Duke, Robinson, Miglioranzi, Hewlett, Invincible (Davis), Sabin, Parkin.
Barnsley: Marriott, Austin, Morgan, Flynn, Gibbs, Betsy, Lumsdon (Bertos), Jones, Gorre, Sheron, Dyer.
Attendance: 5,702

Other titles published by Tempus

Don Rogers The Authorised Biography
PETER MATTHEWS

One of the greatest players ever to have graced Swindon Town's County
Ground, Don Rogers was an exciting winger who terrorised defences up
and down the country, cementing his place in the club's folklore by scoring
two goals in Town's 1969 League Cup final victory over Arsenal. He later
moved to Crystal Palace where he became an instant hero, narrowly missing
out on a full England cap.
0 7524 3293 1

Swindon Town Football Club 100 Greats
DICK MATTICK

Spanning over a century of Swindon Town's history, this illustrated guide to
the club's greatest players cannot fail to thrill Swindon fans young and old.
From the Southern League days there are legendary characters like Billy Silto
and Harold Fleming; Bert Head's youthful promotion winners of the 1960s
are represented by the likes of Mike Summerbee and there are also some of
the players who made Swindon's dream of Premiership football a reality.
0 7524 2714 8

Joker in the Pack The Ernie Hunt Story
CHRIS WESTCOTT

Ernie Hunt was one of football's great extroverts, a player with a happy
goalscoring knack who endeared himself to supporters throughout his career.
Beginning his career at Swindon, he was a key member of the side that put
the club on the football map in the 1960s, and later enjoyed spell at Wolves
and Coventry City, for whom he scored the famous 'donkey' free-kick goal
witnessed by millions on BBC's *Match of the Day*.
0 7524 3271 0

Swindon Town Football Club
RICHARD MATTICK

With its rich assortment of action shots, team groups, player portraits, cartoons,
programme covers and other significant items of memorabilia, this book
charts the history of Swindon Town Football Club from its earliest
amateur days up to the side of 1999/2000. Chronicling lows and highs
such as the nightmare of re-election and Town's meteoric rise from Division
Four to the Premiership, it is an essential read for all Swindon fans.
0 7524 2093 3

If you are interested in purchasing other books published by Tempus, or in case you have difficulty finding
any Tempus books in your local bookshop, you can also place orders directly through our website
www.tempus-publishing.com